a JOURNEY
of LOVE,
FAITH, and
REDEMPTION

SIMON & SCHUSTER

New York   London   Toronto   Sydney   New Delhi

SHARE
MY
LIFE

KEM

with David Ritz

Simon & Schuster
1230 Avenue of the Americas
New York, NY 10020

First Simon & Schuster hardcover edition April 2023

SIMON & SCHUSTER and colophon are registered trademarks
of Simon & Schuster, Inc.

For information about special discounts for bulk purchases, please contact Simon
& Schuster Special Sales at 1-866-506-1949 or business@simonandschuster.com.

The Simon & Schuster Speakers Bureau can bring authors to your live event. For
more information or to book an event, contact the Simon & Schuster Speakers
Bureau at 1-866-248-3049 or visit our website at www.simonspeakers.com.

Interior design by Joy O'Meara @ Creative Joy Designs

Manufactured in the United States of America

1 3 5 7 9 10 8 6 4 2

Library of Congress Cataloging-in-Publication Data has been applied for.

ISBN 978-1-9821-9124-5
ISBN 978-1-9821-9127-6 (ebook)

To my loving and devoted mother and father,
Elizabeth and Erick Hardy

My beautiful children,
Troi, Alex, Laylah, Kristoffer, Trinity, and Israel

And my queen, my bride, my wife,
Erica

FOREWORD

———

I am fortunate to have known Kem for some time and have been, like many, mesmerized by his talent. *Share My Life* is a compelling, candid examination of a great artist that is both surprising and inspirational. The reader learns more about Kem the public figure but, more importantly, Kem the man is revealed.

There is an honesty, a purity in Kem's body of work. This book tells us why. It is a story that begins with dysfunction and failure and then, through discipline and faith, ends with achievement and hope. Kem shares with us, in an honest and riveting way, his life journey from disabling addiction to widespread artistic and commercial success. I see more clearly now the connection between that journey and the music for which he is better known. Great art too frequently comes from those who have experienced great pain. Great artists use that dislocation to inspire them and to brand in a unique way the work that is theirs. I often wondered what the source of Kem's artistry was. After reading this book, it is now clear to me. There is a direct line between his life and his art.

In becoming familiar with the painful parts of Kem's narrative, I'd like to think that that component of his life is unique to him. Unfortunately, it is not so. Too many—particularly people of color—struggle with a society that is too often unfair and unjust. Too few have the discipline or the opportunities to overcome the impact of that which is ingrained in this nation. This is not to make excuses. Kem does not. There is the need for individual responsibility. He accepts that, as I do. But there is also the need for societal responsibility; the country must maximize the chances of success for all its citizens by fairly making opportunities available to all. Our society must also recognize that a life is not solely defined by actions that, while negative in nature, can be ameliorated by understanding and second chances. A person cannot only be defined by his worst. We all must be given the chance to be our best.

That is the strength of *Share My Life* and the man whose story it tells. It is a redemptive tale and one that should serve both as inspiration to those in need or distress, and a call for support from those more fortunate. I'd like to say it is a uniquely American story, that Kem's ultimate success was preordained. It is not. His journey mirrors the lives of too many others. Not adequately nurtured as a child, making bad choices on his own, he led a life that could have gone in a completely different direction. For too many others—forgotten by us—that is their fate. Kem's drive, combined with the talent we have all come to know, made his journey, unfortunately, a unique one. There is value in understanding this. There is the need to find ways to support those less talented, but who desire to lead productive lives. To see who the troubled young boy who Kem was become the Kem we are moved by today is a life lesson for America. His life is a demonstration that positive change is almost always possible. It is never likely, however, where people are defined too soon and consigned to lead lives based on early dysfunction.

Share My Life is a story of hope, of redemption. As honest and searing as it is, it is not a story that is only personal in nature. My hope is that as we now listen to the artist in full bloom, we will also hear the young boy and young man whose voices we are exposed to for the first time in the book. They are one and the same person. So are so many others. America must come to know this.

—Eric Holder

SHARE
MY
LIFE

1

NINETEEN

I had dropped out of high school. After I had disappeared for weeks, my father wouldn't let me return. He was permanently kicking me out to protect my mother, who was a recovering alcoholic. My presence would only make her worse. She didn't want to see me. That was hard to hear, but it was even harder to argue with—so I didn't. I stayed silent. I had no defense. I was drinking and drugging and had no intention to stop.

My friend Sam slipped me into the basement of his house, where he said I could sleep in a crawl space under the stairs, so that if his folks came down, they wouldn't see me. The basement had a beige linoleum floor. On the walls were family pictures, including Sam's dad in an army uniform. On the rear wall was a large mirror, the perfect backdrop to their neatly arranged full-service bar. Glass shelves were stocked with brand names like Johnnie Walker and Jack Daniel's. There were multicolored glasses that suggested another era. Sitting on the bar itself was an oversized bottle of Canadian Club.

I went right for it. Hard liquor was a rare treat. I was usually stoned on cheap wine and malt liquor. I downed the whiskey in no time and headed for the crawl space. My small frame adjusted to the tight quarters. The booze flooded me with warmth. I had to rearrange some boxes to squeeze into the space. My brain was barely functioning. That was my aim. Quiet the confusion in my head. Descend into darkness. Numb out. Get through the night so the next day I could find something—beer, wine, or weed—to beat back the monotony of doing nothing and going nowhere.

As much as I appreciated the space Sam provided, survival meant going somewhere else. Since I was broke, the next step up from the crawl space was a rescue shelter. Over the vast landscape of urban and suburban Detroit, I lived in a dozen such places. Even there, I managed to mess things up. No one was willing to put up with my unruly behavior. Forced out of one shelter, I flopped to another.

My spirit had been drained dry by defeat. I hadn't graduated from high school. My senior year had been an emotional, alcoholic fog. I'd gotten nowhere with the one talent I seemed to have: music. The only thing I excelled at was undercutting myself at every turn. My relationship with my parents was in ruins and my only friends were pretty much like me—outliers living on the edge. My social life consisted of nothing more than hanging out with winos and potheads. I couldn't imagine having a girlfriend. I was in absolutely no condition to maintain a romantic relationship. I stole. I lied. I'd become a full-time conniver, sinking into a quicksand of self-loathing.

One morning in early spring, I woke up in a park with the hope of getting high. I went to see a guy I'll call Fletch, a fellow addict I had met at a shelter who had managed to move back into his folks' home. He was a friendly man, mentally challenged and hooked on crack. Our mission was to cop. To do so, he took the keys to his mother's New Yorker. He knew a blood bank where our blood would yield enough cash to satisfy his dealer. We were joined in this effort by one of Fletch's associates—another crackhead. As we drove through the city streets to the blood bank, I realized I had a problem. I had no driver's license. I had lost it because of DWIs. In fact, I had no ID at all. That meant no giving blood. And no giving blood meant no dope.

"No worries," said Fletch. "Stay in the car while we cop. We'll get enough for you."

He and his buddy entered the blood bank and sold their blood. I waited for them to return. Ten minutes. Thirty minutes. An hour. Clearly, they weren't coming back. When I went to find them, I spotted a rear exit and understood what had happened. Rather than share the fruits of their labor, they'd run over to the crack man without me. In fact, Fletch was in such in a hurry, he had forgotten to take the car keys. So, in a state of righteous indignation, I got behind the wheel and peeled off.

I consoled myself by downing a bottle of Richards Wild Irish Rose, nicknamed "bum's brew." The wine lit me up. The day had turned gray; the sky was covered with low-hanging clouds heavy with moisture. When the rain came down, I opened the sunroof. The rain felt great. I felt great. I was speeding along the Lodge Freeway, leaving down-and-dirty Detroit and flying high to the evergreen bliss of Bloomfield Hills, the fancy burb where I'd try to buy more wine. But how could I do that? I was broke, but like most addicts I didn't let that unfortunate fact bother me for long. All that mattered was the feeling of the rain hitting my face and the smooth ride of this plush New Yorker. I didn't know what time it was. Didn't know what day it was. Didn't really care. Fueled by the bum's brew, my brain was running a million miles a minute. I exited the freeway by making a couple of crazy turns. Before I knew it, I was slamming into a car and careening into a ditch. I was trapped inside a stolen car; being drunk didn't help. The rain got heavier. My heart was hammering to the point of explosion. I closed my eyes, hoping it was all a dream. But the scream of sirens interfered with my fantasy. The woman driver in the other car was bruised but alive. I was hauled off to jail.

As I rode in the back of the cop car, the title of one samba-swaying Brazilian song, "A Day in the Life of a Fool," hit home. Except that *fool* was too kind a word. *Fuckup* was more fitting. The drunken car wreck, the injured woman, this catastrophe—all of it pointed to the collapse of my character. Maybe it was strange to have a song pop up in my head during a disaster, but music had always been there as a far-off light in the fog. Now, though, the fog had only thickened.

The first twenty-three years of my life are the hardest to decipher because I was emotionally unconscious. To render my story effectively, I need to revisit the past. The crazy dysfunction of my early life has always troubled me. I find myself wanting to see through the misery and mystery of that dysfunction. I want to understand why and how it all happened. When I imagine the process of wading through those years, I see myself back at the keyboard, sitting for hours on end in search of the lost chord—or lost time.

I've gone from being a painfully shy kid bent on self-destruction to being someone who performs original songs in front of an arena overflowing with appreciative fans.

My story is a tale soaked in the blues.

My blues, like everyone's blues, begin in the long ago and far away.

They connect to my mother's blues, and her mother's blues. Those connections are rhythmic. That rhythm is deep and historical, a rhythm without end.

2

THE VOICE OF SILENCE

My mother, Elizabeth, known as Liz, is the daughter of Katherine Owens.

My grandmother was a survivor. A force of nature. Angry. Powerful.

Her past was a mystery. She never discussed it with any of us. Before marrying Mom's father, Tom (nicknamed TO), there was another man with whom she had five sons. My mother never knew her half brothers. They were lost in the mist of a story that remained untold. Secret lives. Secret losses. Secret traumas. Secrets inside secrets. The fact that my grandmother gave birth to five children before birthing another eight with TO astounds me. Today, at seventy-three, Mom expresses empathy for her mother, a pretty young girl who had no protection from the wiles of men. She suffered greatly, and in suffering her only refuge was silence.

Katherine couldn't stay in one place for long. Sharecropping in rural Tennessee, the family moved from one man's land to another's because she would not tolerate disrespect from anyone. She talked back to her abusive bosses. She stood tall. What does it take for a single mother to raise a brood of children and not fall apart? Her faith was greater than her fear.

My grandmother's faith was rooted in Pentecostal principles. In the country, those principles remained unchallenged. They were all the family knew. Mom's dad had been studying to be a Baptist minister. But that made no difference to my grandmother. She refused to leave the Pentecostal church. All eight of their children, including my mom, were forced to attend Rock Temple, where, she was convinced, the Holy Ghost manifested the one and only true God.

One of the telling descriptions of my mother's childhood came in a four-word saying she often used:

"Silence has a voice."

That sentence struck me deeply. I might say that this book speaks with the voice of silence.

I am a person prone to silence. So is my mother. And, according to her, so was my grandmother, who lived to age ninety-four. I come from a long line of people who are far more comfortable with silence than with the spoken word. Silence adds to our mystery, and maybe even to our allure. But this profound and abiding silence, which marks the generations of my grandmother, my mother, and myself, also serves as a mask. Facts remain hidden. Feelings are suppressed. Communication is stifled.

———————

My mother's life began in the spring of 1950 in West Tennessee, where she, her seven siblings, and TO and Katherine worked the land outside the tiny village of Bells.

Mom loved the land. It was her version of the Garden of Eden. No poverty, no fears, no sense of a world beyond the one she saw. Her innocence was complete. If evil existed, it was far off.

She remembers the first seven years of her life as a time of peace: misty sunrises and golden sunsets, the sensation of changing seasons—the warmth of summer, the chill of fall, the frost of winter, the fresh blossoms of spring. Nature's steady rhythm brought security. The fragrance of wildflowers, the taste of fresh corn, the sounds of sparrows and bluebirds. An idyllic world. The reality of the economic exploitation inherent in sharecropping might have been brewing in the minds of her older brothers, but Mom was just a child who found delight in the natural world.

Rock Temple was a Pentecostal congregation where blood-washed believers let the gifts of the spirit flow freely. The full-throated gospel was preached from the word and expressed in song. Through the faithful, the Holy Ghost spoke in tongues. My mother drank it all in. It served as a source of comfort. She accepted these practices as God-given. Certainty gave her strength. Night followed day. Sunshine followed rain. My mother and grandmother went on worshipping God one way and one way only.

The extreme restrictions of the Pentecostal faith had no immediate impact on the Owens family, who, living in the country, were already detached from urban America. They were not allowed to dance, but even if they had been, there were no dance halls or night-clubs to frequent. Popular music was off-limits, but who had money to buy records or a radio? Movies were prohibited, but the closest cinema was in Jackson, sixteen miles away. Besides, who had money for a ticket?

TO never lived with Katherine and the children. My mother called him the Mystery Man. His absence was a disturbing fact of her early life. She also knew that her father had been married before. The kids from his first marriage would sometimes come by to visit their dad's second wife. It was strange and unexplained. When TO did show up, it was usually for the holidays. His comings and goings became part of the routine of Mom's young life. Katherine Owens assumed her role as matriarch. By necessity, she was a strict disciplinarian. By conviction, she was a fervent believer. She felt directed by God to obey his commandments—and make her offspring do the same.

And then, in 1957, when Mom turned seven, everything changed. The family moved from the country to the city.

3

EAST OF EDEN

For Elizabeth Ann Owens, Jackson, Tennessee, her family's new home, was east of Eden. She had been expelled from the garden, not through any fault of her own, but because of her mother's restless and enigmatic nature.

That critical move to Jackson came without warning. In the middle of the night, with the help of a relative, all the family's worldly belongings were loaded into the back of a pickup and off they went.

Was there a dispute between my grandmother and the landowners? Was there an ugly confrontation? Mom wasn't told. She couldn't ask because asking wasn't allowed. All she could do was scramble to pack up and, with her mother and siblings, head out into the night.

They arrived in the city of sixty-five thousand, where they settled into a small duplex. The contrast between rich soil and cold concrete was startling. There was no garden, no green fields yielding food. Instead, only frightening uncertainty. My grandmother found work as a domestic, holding down two jobs at once.

In Jackson, Pentecostals worshipped outside the mainstream, meaning that Mom found herself doubly ostracized. She was a Black country girl living in a segregated city ruled by whites. She was also set apart in the Black community, where her mother would not accept the predominant Baptist denomination of her own husband.

Every Sunday, Katherine transported her children twenty-five miles back to Rock Temple, the small sanctuary that remained their spiritual home.

In the city, the kids were left to fend for themselves. Everything was different. Mom was afraid but couldn't say so. Children were to be seen and not heard. There was a new school, a radically new environment, in an urban setting she'd never seen before. How to cope? Her older brothers were long gone. Her remaining siblings were all girls except their younger brother. Mom was the fourth youngest and the child the closest to Katherine, who may have sensed Liz shared her resourcefulness. That coping mechanism had everything to do with using sheer determination and self-reliance to overcome obstacles. She may have also known how closely my mother watched her. At the same time, my grandmother was neither affectionate nor inclined to praise her children. Like all kids, Mom hungered for affection and praise. Katherine's main concern was protecting her brood.

And yet the single thing that traumatized Mom most—and perhaps traumatized Katherine as well—was something for which there's no protection: poverty. This was the ugly and inevitable fact that, for the first time, Mom had to face. Living in the country was all about abundance. Living in the city was all about scarcity. Suddenly there wasn't enough.

My grandmother, my mother, and her siblings stayed in Jackson only two years before heading out to Nashville. There was no advance notice. But there was, at least, an obvious explanation. For the first time in Mom's life, her parents would be permanently living under the same roof. Except the permanence was short-lived.

The year was 1961. A Freedom Riders' bus was firebombed in Alabama, where the governor declared martial law. The Ku Klux Klan acted with impunity. Newly elected, President Kennedy promised to put a man on the moon by the end of the decade. And Ray Charles topped the charts with "Hit the Road Jack."

In Nashville, eleven-year-old Liz Owens knew none of this. Mom was still prohibited from going to the movies or listening to any music the church did not sanction. Although Nashville is the capital of and largest city in Tennessee, her life remained closed off to current events and political considerations. Rock Temple, the country Pentecostal church, was replaced by King's Temple, the city Pentecostal church. The Baptist church, where my grandfather had begun to preach, was off-limits, even to his own children. Grandma would have it no other way.

All children want Mommy and Daddy to be together. Mom was no different. She prayed for her reunited family to stay reunited. But because her father was as secretive and stubbornly silent as her mother, hope was all Mom had. Hope didn't last long. Unspoken rage hung over Katherine's and TO's heads like dark clouds. The storm was always about to erupt. Where was the anger coming from? Was it the phone calls Granddad was getting from women in his congregation? Was it because his wife was working two jobs at once and came home every night tired and cross? Mom didn't know what to think, but she knew what to say. Nothing. Just keep quiet and observe. Then came the evening that Mom saw something that stayed with her forever.

4

EMASCULATION

Mom looked into the small room where her parents slept. Grandpa was sitting on the side of their double bed. He was wearing an undershirt and boxer shorts. Grandma had scissors in her hand. She took the scissors and, like a seamstress, carefully cut around the band of his shorts until they fell away from his body. For a moment, Mom wondered if Grandma was going to stab him with the scissors, but the threat of violence wasn't there. My grandmother had already committed a murderous act to his manhood. She had stripped him bare. He simply sat there. He didn't utter a word. He was rendered powerless. Although Mom didn't really understand the dynamics behind what she was witnessing, one thing was clear: it was her mother, not her father, who possessed the power. Right then and there, the relationship between my grandparents, always fragile, collapsed.

The very night of the clothes-cutting incident, Katherine took Mom with her to search for a place to live. She was leaving her husband and taking the kids. They found a single room with a kitchen and stayed there until she was able to rent larger quarters. Never again would my grandmother even entertain the notion of reconciling with my grandfather.

On Saturday nights my mother sought solace at King's Temple, where she helped prepare Sunday meals for the congregants. It was a safe place, until it wasn't. The minister's son, a married man with three children, was interested in pretty little Liz Owens. He was not shy about expressing that interest. He made overtly sexual advances toward her that went on for months.

Mom finally found the courage to tell Grandma the ugly truth: Reverend's son wouldn't leave her alone. He'd tried coaxing her into his car to take her to a motel. He kept grabbing her, feeling her, threatening her if she wouldn't give in.

Grandma listened carefully. After a long pause she told Mom not to mention it to Reverend.

Mom was flabbergasted. Wouldn't Reverend want to know what his son was up to? And wouldn't her own mother want to protect her from a predator?

Yet all Katherine told her daughter was to keep her mouth shut and mind her own business. Suddenly the one spot that had always been safe—church—became a spot that put her in danger. She couldn't go back, and she didn't. No more Saturday nights spent preparing Sunday dinners. She wanted her mom to say, "I'll go to Reverend and give him a piece of my mind. I'll set things straight. No daughter of mine needs to go through something like this." But she never heard those words. Instead, she absorbed a dangerous idea: my grandmother's words made Mom feel she wasn't worth protecting. She felt "less than." It was a feeling that shaped the rest of her life.

My grandmother never brought it up again. Consequently, Mom suffered in silence. Her only real friend, a boy named Robert, was someone she could confide in. Robert was cool, but he was just a kid like Mom. They had a natural brother-sister rapport. He could commiserate with my mother's dilemma, but he could hardly take on the preacher's son who was making her life miserable.

School was another place of struggle for my mother. When she got to Pearl High in Nashville, class became an issue. Many of the students were the children of doctors and lawyers. Because Liz Owens was both pretty and smart and often singled out by the teachers as an exemplary student, she was bullied by her female classmates.

She didn't see herself as pretty. When she was in eighth grade, she was in a car accident. Her head smashed into the windshield. Stitches were required. That's when one of her sisters said, "Liz, you're not pretty anymore." Even though there was no disfigurement, Mom took those words to heart. She saw herself as homely.

The bullying continued. Some of the girls teased her for wearing unfashionable clothes. Some resented her for being reserved. Because her Pentecostal upbringing had excluded all popular culture, she had little in common with the other girls. What did she know about Sonny and Cher or the Supremes? What could she say about *The Sound of Music* or *Doctor Zhivago*, movies she was prohibited from seeing? What did she know about sex?

Mom's sexual awakening was hardly an awakening at all. It was an act of defiance. It happened with an air force cadet who was eager to fly. Mom wasn't eager. Just curious. And after years of being dominated by her mother's heavy-handed orthodoxy, she was more than ready to rebel.

5

BIRTH OF SHAME

It was my mother's second sexual encounter that brought me into this world. The circumstances surrounding my birth on July 23, 1967, were scandalous.

Mom and her sister Tina were working at an A&W restaurant as waitresses. Mom was sixteen. She didn't mind the job. Even as she rebelled against the dogma of the Pentecostal church, she maintained an ironclad work ethic. Mom saw work as a good thing. Mostly, men didn't mess with her. She was barely a hundred pounds and didn't see herself as sexy. But one man did.

Turned out that man was an algebra teacher at Pearl High, where my mother would be a senior the following year. His name was Jesse Nance Jr. He was thirty-two. When he ordered his burger and fries, he was exceedingly friendly. He returned a few days later, and then a few days after that, each time growing friendlier. His intentions were obvious. He seemed nice, but Mom wasn't interested. After all, he taught in the same school she attended. That put her off. But nothing could deter Jesse. He had no wife or children and lived with his brother. He assured her everything was all right. His father was a minister. He himself was college educated. He was also soft-spoken and a man of few words. That made Mom comfortable, since the other people in her life—especially her own parents—were hardly big talkers. And even though she knew it was wrong to give in to the advances of a man twice her age, not to mention a teacher at the school where next year she'd be graduating, she followed his lead.

He was smooth. He was determined. He was insistent. He got Mom over to his house on a day when his brother was gone. Later in her life she described the experience as passionless. It was an act of rebellion, a way for Mom to flout her own mother's strict rules.

It was not her intention to carry on with Jesse. When she saw him at school, she nervously looked the other way. Other times, when he saw her walking in his direction, he avoided her. Jesse wanted nothing more to do with her. As she'd expected, once he made his conquest, he never sought her out again. Mom thought things would go back to normal. Except they didn't. All hell broke loose.

When Mom found out she was pregnant with me, her sister told their mother, who flew into a rage. She insisted that Mom march into King's Temple, stand before the congregation, and confess her sin. Liz refused. If she had sinned, that was her business. And besides, she didn't see it as sin. She saw it as an older man who had seduced a young girl. Katherine saw it as shameful, and while Mom might have beat back the notion of sin, shame was something she couldn't escape.

6

MOTHER AND MOM

During the early months of her pregnancy, Mom heard her mother speaking to her sister about a schoolmate.

"At least she's not stupid like Liz," said Katherine.

The thought made Mom furious, while her mother grew more furious with her. That fury, true to the Owens family style, remained unspoken. It was Katherine's scornful looks that expressed her anger. But then, during Mom's sixth month of pregnancy, her mother couldn't contain her rage and forcibly struck her daughter with her hands.

That night Mom moved out and went to her father's home. By then Grandpa had a new wife, Martha, who had brought her three children to the marriage. Without a single question, Grandpa gave his daughter shelter. She spent the night on his couch, crying her eyes out. The next morning her mother came to fetch her. Grandma refused to venture inside her ex-husband's home, but Mom saw her sitting in a car by the curb. She went out to see her. Her mother was weeping. No words were spoken, no apologies given. But, again through silence, Mom was made to understand that her mother, despite everything, would help her through the rest of her pregnancy. Mom went back to her mother's home.

When the school confronted Jesse, he lied and claimed that Mom had shown up at his house one day to seduce *him*. The principal believed him. To demonstrate his gallantry, Jesse offered to marry my mother. She flat-out refused. The last thing in the world she wanted was to marry a man she didn't love. She knew Jesse had no love for her. His proposal was a ruse, a sly maneuver to free him of his guilt and allow him to play the part of a stand-up guy.

For all my grandmother's wrath at the notion of her sixteen-year-old daughter giving birth out of wedlock during the summer of 1967, the same summer of smoldering civil unrest, it was my grandmother who cared for me as my primary parent.

As soon as I was old enough to talk, I would call my grandmother "Mother" and her daughter "Mom."

Both women bathed me in love. Obviously, as an infant, I had no awareness of the conflict between them.

Mother wanted to raise me as her own. She liked to say, "This is *my* child." She even filed a statutory rape charge against Jesse. The suit was dropped when Jesse sent a little money, but those payments soon ceased. Jesse vanished from our life. Mom heard about him only through others. He suffered from heart disease and underwent a double bypass operation. He was also imprisoned for molesting a minor. During his incarceration, his heart gave out and he passed away. He was fifty-nine. Mom decided there was no good reason for me to ever know the identity of my biological father, and I can't say his presence was missed. I was under the care of two conscientious women, Mother and Mom.

Mom couldn't go back to Pearl High because of their policy against the admission of single mothers, but she was adamant about pursuing her education. She knew it was the key to her future as an independent woman. Of course, given the gender inequality, the high school had no policy against the admission of young men who had fathered children. Either way, Mom didn't want to go back to Pearl. Pearl was the scene of the scandal surrounding her and Jesse Nance.

In spite of that scandal, Mom doubled down. She enrolled at Central High and graduated with a 4.0 and an honors degree. Her plan was to go straight to college. Because Grandpa's job as minister of Hopewell Missionary Baptist Church came without a salary, he worked at Vanderbilt University in maintenance. He wanted Mom to attend Vanderbilt, but no one could afford the tuition. Instead, she enrolled at Tennessee State.

Katherine Owens didn't understand her daughter's obsession with school. My grandmother was the only member of the family not to attend Mom's high school graduation.

7

OUR FATHER

My mother was smart, curious, and alive with ambition. Working at a local hospital, she met Michael, whom she considered her first real boyfriend, a musician who viewed life creatively. Mom was living at her dad's while Mother was keeping me. Mother forbade Mom to date. Her father was far more liberal.

Later in life Mom discovered a passage, Mathew 11:29, that, as translated by the *Message* Bible, says, "Learn the unforced rhythms of grace." Michael showed her the unforced rhythms of romance.

Around the same time, Mom enrolled at Tennessee State and majored in accounting, where she met fellow student Erick Hardy, who pursued her relentlessly. Michael, who liked to play the field, proved to be unfaithful. Erick proved to be loyal. Erick also had ambition. He was locked into his major in engineering. Erick was Mr. Responsibility. Mr. Dependability. Mr. Intellectual. When Mom stepped away from Michael, Erick stepped in. They started dating in September of 1969 and married three months later.

Why so quickly? Maybe the words that Mother had spoken to her after my birth—"Now no one will ever marry you"—had haunted her. She wanted to show her mother that she was not "less than" or "unwanted" or "tainted." A respectable man with a promising future had proposed. In December of 1969, Erick and Mom officially tied the knot in a ceremony presided over by my grandfather in his Hopewell Missionary Baptist Church. Katherine Owens refused to attend.

———————

I can't remember the battle between Mother and Mom. Though I do remember my grandmother's warmth and care. I can also remember the fright I felt when she took me to her Pentecostal church. Up front was a mural of a white guy nailed to a cross, blood pouring from his hands. The congregation was in hysterics. Sister Betty was crying out with the Holy Ghost. Women were fainting. Men were hollering. I was grabbing Mother's hand. Mother was talking in tongues. Kids were being held over coffins at funerals to kiss the late Sister Mabel on the forehead. For all the love I felt from Mother, church seemed to be anything but a sanctuary of love. It took me a lifetime to get back, as the Beatles say, to where I once belonged.

After Mom and Erick became a unit, Mother was resolute about keeping me, but her daughter wasn't about to back down. Mom never considered leaving me. Erick was silent on the matter. So, at the age of two I was taken from Mother to live with Mom and the only man I would ever call Dad.

Mom and Erick got pregnant a few months after their marriage, but before he could graduate from Tennessee State, he was in a serious car accident, dislocated his hip, and wound up in the hospital for six months. During his recovery, Mom and I lived with my grandfather's family. It was a setback that postponed their future.

My sister Ericka was born May 9, 1971. By June, Dad had recovered. The four of us—me, Ericka, Mom, and Dad—moved to an apartment on Eleventh Street, only doors away from Mom's older sister Marjorie and her family.

That's where, in secretive and uncomfortable ways, I was introduced to sex.

8

THE NAUGHTY AND NASTY

I was four. My playmates were nine or ten. Together, we pretended we were the Jackson 5, who had just exploded on the national scene. Since I was the youngest, I saw myself as Michael. We weren't really singers or dancers, just little kids imitating this fantastic group we'd seen on TV singing "ABC."

Our playing, though, involved more than that. The older kids would touch me, even undress me. There was giggling. There was heavy fondling. There were feelings. There was stimulation. There were smells. There was never penetration, but there were erections. All this was new, exciting, and strange. I didn't even realize it was "wrong" until I made a remark about it to an uncle, who reacted with horror. That's when I first got the idea that sex was wrong. Not just boy-to-boy sex but any sex. The sex play went on for many months, maybe even a year. I felt naughty; I felt intimidated by the bigger boys; I felt small; but mostly I felt shame. Shame, guilt, remorse—all part of the same heavy package that I'd carry around for decades. Sex would not be an easy thing to deal with.

I can't remember when I was made to understand the mechanics of sexual intercourse, but I do remember its neighborhood name: "the nasty." Calling the act "the nasty" is no trivial matter. No one called it "the bonding" or "the beauty" or even "the loving." It was "the nasty," and in my mind, both consciously and unconsciously, it remained "the nasty." Just as there was no adult around to explain that innocent sex play among kids is as natural as breathing, I had no one telling me that calling sexual intimacy "the nasty" was corroding my relationship to sexuality.

9

MAZE OF CONFUSION

In early 1972, Mom became pregnant with her third child. It came at a moment of her life when she was especially vulnerable emotionally.

Mom's friend Robert, her cherished confidant from her childhood years at King's Temple, was passing through Nashville on his way to Vietnam. A doctor's appointment kept her from seeing him. His layover was short, so Mom missed the chance to tell him goodbye and wish him well. Then a month later came the devastating news: Robert had been killed in action. Mom didn't want to believe it. She waited for another call to say it had all been a mistake. There was no way that his twenty-two-year-old life could be over. Mom's mind was a maze of confusion and grief.

Then, at a party with Dad and some of his classmates who had graduated from Tennessee State, Mom was passed a joint. They were celebrating. Dad had just been offered a job as an engineer with Rockwell International in far-off Pontiac, Michigan. Mom should have been happy. But she wasn't. She took a puff of the joint and was disoriented for three days—so disoriented that she couldn't hold down her job at Tennessee State, where she was working as a cafeteria cashier. She couldn't stop crying. She was sent to a doctor, who gave her Valium. But Valium only made things worse.

Dad assured her that all would be well once we got to Pontiac. Pontiac represented prosperity. But in those weeks before moving, those same weeks when Mom broke down, Mother started insisting Mom leave me with her. My grandmother saw me as hers. After all, I called her Mother. Mother dominated. Mother thought that Erick would have preferred to leave me with her—and Mother was probably right.

Yet in this battle between mother and daughter, the daughter prevailed. Whatever else was going on in her life, Mom never considered abandoning me. No one, not even her intimidatingly powerful mother, was going to take her baby from her.

10

SENSITIVE PEOPLE

I was five when we left Tennessee, a turning point in our lives.

The trip felt endless. Dad was driving, Mom riding shotgun; me and my baby sister Ericka were in the back. We were heading to Pontiac, 565 miles away, trading one world for another. The only relief came from the radio, where deejays kept playing a new Marvin Gaye song where he sang about sensitive people. I heard how his voice was filled with longing, but I wasn't sure about the title: "Let's Get It On."

I thought it meant "Let's get on with this trip, let's keep driving, let's keep going until we arrive at this mysterious city that carries the name of a car." The song kept me excited. The groove propelled my excitement. The groove seemed to be pushing us down the highway. If Marvin was excited about singing, I was excited about moving to someplace I'd never seen before.

We moved into Pontiac's Ridgemont Apartments at 183 Ridgemont Drive. Today they would probably be considered projects. But back then, in the early 1970s, they were cool. Unlike our Nashville neighborhood, this one was racially diverse. I liked that. I liked hearing different accents and checking out people whose skin tones were different from my own. White people. Latinos. Asian people. Everyone was represented.

The difference in energy between Nashville and Pontiac was night and day. Pontiac is basically an offshoot of Detroit, and Detroit was all about upward mobility. My dad bought into that aspirational energy. Rockwell International made brakes and axles for Ford, GM, and Chrysler. His job involved travel to other auto plants in Mexico and Brazil.

Soon after we arrived, Mom gave birth to my second sister, Karen, and for the next twelve years, until my third baby sister, Karmen, came along in 1984, our nuclear family was complete.

The Hardy household was tense. My dad wasn't simply strict, he was hostile. Little things bothered him. For example, if I turned on *Soul Train* to watch Sly Stone or the Stylistics, Dad would grumble to himself, "This is nonsense." It wasn't the singers he objected to; it was the dancers. "Those kids should be in school. They should be working on their grades, not showing off their fancy clothes and acting a fool." My father wasn't simply serious about the world; he was *dead* serious. He had no patience for frivolity.

After Karen was born, Mom suffered from postpartum depression. She didn't know how to deal with the tension between her son and her husband. Life with her own mother had never been easy, but a few years into marriage, she felt that she had jumped from the skillet into the fire. Because she had taken her vows seriously, and because she was the mother of three young children, she was not about to leave. But she was miserable. She had considerable empathy for her husband but not enough to mellow her relationship with him. Erick's dad was an alcoholic who had abandoned him. His mom and grandma had spoiled him. His default mode was passive aggression. He couldn't discipline children. That became Mom's job. He remained distant from the day-to-day tasks of raising us.

As a kid, I loved people. I'd walk across the street to talk to a couple of older men who entertained me with stories. Dad didn't like that. He chided me and told me to stay away from strangers. But these men were hardly strangers. They were neighbors. Mom might have stepped in to mitigate the situation, but Mom was on a different course. She was drinking. Like Dad, she loved beer. Beer became their bond. Beer gave them just the right buzz. It took the edge off. Dad was able to manage his drinking, and in the beginning so was Mom. Unlike cocaine or heroin or even pot, beer seemed harmless. What was wrong with kicking back at the end of the day with a little Budweiser? After all, it was the king of beers. This seemingly harmless habit turned out to be pernicious. Mom fooled herself by thinking her drinking was not a problem. That subterfuge went on for years. I bought into it, and so did Dad. Like me, he didn't see it for what it was—an escape from an emotional reality Mom found intolerable. As badly as she was hurting, she didn't say a word to anyone. Just as her mother had never discussed her demons, Mom didn't discuss hers. Once again, feelings remained both unexpressed and suppressed. Deadly silence prevailed.

I was just a kid, running the streets, playing with friends, and doing what little boys do. Nothing too crazy except for the one time my buddy Larry and I nearly blew up his house messing around with a can of Lysol and a cigarette lighter. Fortunately, disaster was averted. When Larry's mother discovered our little experiment, I ran like hell, while my friend got his ass whupped. The fact that Larry lived in a house while we lived in an apartment was my first awareness of social hierarchy. A vivid awareness of class distinction, though, didn't come till later.

A vivid awareness of the opposite sex, however, would come much earlier.

In kindergarten, I found myself crawling under a bathroom stall so I could get in there to hug up on one of my female classmates. My drive for romance—if that's the right word—was already in gear. Or maybe it was an extension of those sex-play scenarios that had happened in Nashville. The startled little girl had no interest. I backed off, but she reported the incident. The principal gave me a note to take home to my mother. I tore up the note. Why incriminate myself?

Soon after we moved to Pontiac, my folks hired a teenage girl to babysit my sisters and me. We arrived to find her babysitting another child, a young girl, who was around the same age as me. After my sisters fell asleep, the babysitter gave me and the other child explicit instructions about a sexual act she wanted us to perform. The girl was into it, but I wasn't. She and the babysitter shamed me because I wouldn't participate.

Afterward, the babysitter threatened to beat my brains out if I told anyone.

She didn't have to worry. I was too scared and too ashamed to say a word about it to anybody.

Shame. There it was again, relentlessly playing its part. It said, "You're not man enough. You're a pussy for not getting with that girl."

———————

Shame seemed to find me everywhere. My father never hit me, but he shamed me for being, in his words, "a knucklehead." He was verbally abusive. If Mom's mother made her feel "less than," my dad made me feel the same. A day didn't pass when I wasn't called a "sorry ass" or a "dumb shit." Mom once said emotional abuse is far worse than physical abuse, because with the former you don't even know where you've been hit.

Mom's way of escaping abuse was not to leave the marriage but to fight for her independence. That meant going back to school. Dad was against it. He clung to the timeworn notion that a woman's place is in the home. But the home was suffocating Mom. To stay sane, she had to get out and pursue her education. That led her to enroll at Wayne State University in downtown Detroit. And that meant her children would also be going to school in Detroit, a change that would have a huge impact on me.

Although my sisters and I got along fine, I couldn't shake the feeling that I was on my own. My sisters forged a relationship with Dad that was very different from mine. Whenever the topic of our childhood comes up, Ericka never fails to describe our mom as distant and cold, even unapproachable, whereas she considers Dad more emotionally available. The Katherine-and-Liz mother-daughter dynamic endured. Ericka experienced Dad's love in a way that I never did—and she gravitated toward it.

11

SUMMERTIME BLUES

Most kids love summer. No school, no homework, no rigid routine. Ride your bike. Play till it's dark. Eat lots of ice cream. Run free.

Starting at age nine and continuing for several summers, I didn't associate summer with that sense of freedom. If anything, I felt imprisoned. My dad decided to send me and my sisters to West Palm Beach, Florida, during our summer breaks. We would stay with his mother.

No explanations were given, and of course, no questions could be asked. Mom and Dad said we'd have a great time. That wasn't always the case.

The best part was the train ride. When I wasn't running up and down the aisles, I stayed glued to the window. We headed south to Ohio before rolling over the hills and horse country of Kentucky and Tennessee. Night fell, but I was too excited to sleep. I saw moonlit Alabama and early morning Georgia. Baked in sunlight, the flatlands of Florida spread out before me like a dream. It all seemed wonderful before it all turned scary.

Along with her extended family, Dad's mom, Maurice, lived in low-rise projects. Her husband was long gone. The heat was suffocating, the humidity even worse. Within hours, my face and arms were covered with bug bites. I couldn't stop scratching.

The apartments were colorless and confining. The complex felt not only walled off from the rest of the world but dangerous. During our first week, I was playing outside when I saw two women get into a fight a few feet away from me. "Go get my heater," one of them told her son. He raced into the apartment and raced back out holding a paper bag. She reached into the bag to grab a gun. Frightened to death, we ran back into Grandma's apartment. I half expected to be shot in the back. The altercation was finally defused, but I stayed scared for a week. Every time I saw the gun-toting woman, I ran in the opposite direction.

I didn't feel entirely comfortable around Dad's Florida family. I'm not sure how my sisters felt. But they must have related to Grandma Maurice more than I did. As adults, they would wind up moving to Florida to be near her. Perhaps she provided the sense of warmth they missed from our mom. Grandma Maurice did her best to call me out of my isolation when I stayed holed up in the bedroom. I was miserable during those Florida summers. I felt abandoned by Mom and Dad.

As I struggled to fall asleep, late at night I would wonder why we had been shipped off. Why didn't they want us around? In the distance, the shrill whistle of a train reminded me of the great distance between me and my parents. I wanted to go home but I wasn't allowed to say so.

One morning, I was sitting in the backyard of my grandmother's unit when I decided to finally vent my feelings. I let my sisters know how much I hated being in Florida. How there was nothing to do. How the heat was driving me crazy. How Dad's family didn't really care about us. How everything sucked.

The second I got through ranting, I heard a scream that chilled me to the bone.

It was my grandmother. Without realizing it, I had done all my complaining underneath her second-story bedroom window, which she'd left wide open. She'd heard every word I said. Her tirade against me was a hundred times worse than mine against her. She called me ungrateful. She said I had absolutely no sense of appreciation. How could I fail to acknowledge all she'd done for us? Didn't I see how lucky I was to have this Florida vacation free of charge?

No, I didn't feel lucky, and no, I was not appreciative, and yes, I would have loved to get the hell out. But I just stood there and took it. Answering back would have only made things worse.

After that, things grew more tense. I never knew if she reported my attitude back to my folks, but I had a feeling she let my father know. The next summer, when I asked my father whether we were being sent to Florida again, he answered, "You already know you're going back. And this time you should show some gratitude."

That next summer I made a friend. I'll call him Joe. He and I would play ball and take walks. Anything to get away from the projects. Sometimes we'd go to a convenience store and buy sodas and pickled eggs. Sometimes we'd hang out at the basketball court when the older kids were hooping. Joe was a good pal.

That's why I didn't understand why, on an afternoon when I was watering the small patch of grass in front of Grandma's building, Joe showed up with another kid to taunt me. They called me names, all having to do with my short stature and dark skin. Prejudice regarding skin color is something African Americans know all too well. But this was the first time it was aimed directly at me. My reaction surprised me. I took the hose I was holding and wielded it to beat up both boys. That hardly turned me into a fighter, but it did show me that, when provoked, I could fly into a fury. I wasn't unhappy when I bloodied Joe's nose.

Those summer months dragged on without relief. My parents never spoke to us while we were in Florida. I was assured my grandmother discussed our well-being when they called, but they never asked to speak to us kids. It would have made life easier if they had.

Some relief came when Dad's brother, Uncle Billy, took us to spend a day at the beach. He even drove us up to Disney World once. Up until that point, I'd only seen Mickey Mouse on TV.

For all the confusion I experienced in Florida, there were times when my family showed me love.

Grandma Maurice always had a pot on the stove. Collard greens, lima beans, ham hocks, chitterlings—her cooking was off the chain. She and her mother, my great-grandmother, whom I called Nanny, had worked as domestics in the homes of wealthy white people in Palm Beach. They turned me on to other treats like apricot nectar, oysters Rockefeller, and fresh bagels with cream cheese and lox. I figured we were the only ones in the projects getting our culinary groove on like this.

Despite these occasional pleasures, the daily do-nothing summer grind got to me. I was desperate for an escape. I thought escape might come in the form of a bottle of Dristan I found in Grandma's bedroom. It was a pathetic attempt to alter my mood and get high. The attempt didn't work. So I turned to other means.

I noticed a gallon of Smirnoff vodka that sat on the floor of the closet that housed the water heater. The temptation was too great to resist. On a hundred-degree afternoon, I poured the vodka into a sixteen-ounce glass and added orange juice. No one had instructed me on how to make a screwdriver. I'd never heard the term. I just did it.

Just then a friend of one of my aunts, a woman in her early twenties, walked into the kitchen and caught me. She didn't seem to care. She took a taste herself and said it was too strong. Not for me. I downed it, and within minutes, my head was spinning and my stomach churning. The combination of the unbearable heat, the stifling humidity, and the eighty-proof booze made me seriously sick. In trying to escape reality, I made myself only more miserable.

In the coming years, the stimulants would change. I would change. I would grow increasingly dependent on an assortment of methods to escape the inescapable. Little did I know, at age eleven or twelve, right down there in Florida, I had innocently begun venturing into a swamp where hungry alligators were ready to eat me alive.

12

THE LONG WAY HOME

I was always glad to get out of Florida. But back home in Pontiac, life was less than cheerful. I was thirteen and set to start middle school at Michigan Institute for Child Development and had no idea what to expect. It wasn't until I was an adult that my mother explained how I wound up there.

Mom had to get her degree. It was her only escape hatch. She'd put her foot down and said that she'd be going to Wayne State, a university in Detroit. So it was in Detroit that she found us a school—Michigan Institute for Child Development, a private academy with a good reputation. Dad was willing to pay the tuition but refused to buy a second car.

The result was a rough routine, but I liked the twenty-five-mile ride from Pontiac to Detroit. In winter, we started off early in the morning, when it was still dark. Mom got behind the wheel of our old Plymouth Satellite, first dropping off Dad at Rockwell. Then we drove all the way down Woodward Avenue, through blue-collar neighborhoods and past business districts where I'd suddenly see a larger-than-life snowman standing in front of a Mercedes-Benz dealership. I loved that snowman, loved looking at the big houses in the rich suburbs of Bloomfield and Birmingham, loved the feeling of security that came from Mom. She knew how to drive. She knew where to go. She exuded confidence. She turned up the volume on the radio—Kenny Rogers's "The Gambler," Peaches & Herb's "Reunited," the Pointer Sisters' "He's So Shy." Mom made sure I and my sisters were dropped off at school on time before she dashed over to Wayne State for her classes. At three thirty, I knew she'd be there to get us—she was never late—and then we were back on the road, racing over to Rockwell to collect Dad and drive home.

Mom's first major was accounting. That seemed the most practical route. But thanks to the wisdom of several professors who took an interest in her, she switched to marketing. They saw her strength in sales. One teacher even put her in touch with Fordham University in New York City, where, given her good grades, she was offered a full scholarship. But because Dad was traveling for his work, often for weeks at a time, she had to assume primary responsibility for us. Fordham sounded great, but Fordham would never happen.

Mom didn't drink during the day, but as soon as she got home she went right for the beer. As a kid, I hardly noticed, but it must have registered subconsciously because eventually beer became my main buzz. Always sipping on a Budweiser, Mom cooked dinner, cleaned up, supervised the kids' homework, did her own homework, and finally, exhausted, fell into bed.

Later we would all learn that there are many forms of drunks:

those who black out, fall out, or act out. Mom was in the category of those who remain functional. It took her over a decade to realize that functional alcoholics are among the most dangerous. In the absence of high drama, they can stay in denial until they wind up drinking themselves to death.

13

BOURGEOIS ET NOIR

Much of my school experience mirrored my mother's. I felt out of place. Michigan Institute was all-Black, and, though I didn't know the word then, it was bougie. I attended the school from ages ten to thirteen. The kids sitting in the early morning assembly had nicer clothes than I did. Many were the children of doctors, lawyers, and professors. The hip kids wore black suede boots called jingles. Others had snow-white Nikes without a smudge. That little polo man was embroidered on their pink shirts. My clothes paled in comparison. My $1.99 Kmart sneaker specials and my Sears Toughskins jeans with the patches in the knees made me feel worthless.

Those feelings only intensified when the school founder, Roslyn Murray, took the stage. Ms. Murray, a highly accomplished public figure, owned several private schools in the area. She was an imposing woman, a grande dame who wore extravagant outfits—satin dresses, wide-brimmed feathered hats, fancy high-heeled shoes. She spoke like an actress. She was fluent in several languages. She comported herself like a queen. She talked about the high standards of her great institution.

"This is Michigan Institute for Child Development," she said, "with an emphasis on the word *development. Development* means 'growth,' and growth is something we expect each and every one of our students to experience."

As a short kid, the only growth that interested me was getting taller.

"Academic growth," the headmistress continued, "entails diligent study. Many of you come from privileged homes. With privilege comes responsibility."

Privileged homes? What did that mean? Her inflated language left me behind. I felt lost and alone. The sting of classism hurt. I belonged to a lower class than these other Black kids. As the days passed by, I realized being small of stature was enough to invite ridicule. I was also teased for being dark skinned. Both the boys and the girls with lighter hues seemed to be more popular. They had status. I had nothing.

For all the talk of academic excellence, the school was a hotbed of sexual dysfunction. During that first semester, I became friends with a boy who had caught the eye of a female teacher. She was smitten with him. He was thirteen. She was thirty. She stood outside the men's room and handed out tissue paper, instructing us to clean our private parts. The amount of tissue paper she allotted wasn't equal. She made it clear that those she thought of as having small private parts would be given only a single sheet. She gave me a single sheet. She gave my friend five sheets. Adding to the humiliation was the fact that she did all this in plain sight. We bearers of single sheets were humiliated in front of our peers. She also didn't hesitate to tell my friend, in my presence, that she had sexual dreams about him. I don't think her seduction was successful, but it was frightening and confusing to witness.

Sexual inappropriateness was rampant. Students would sneak into back rooms, where skirts were lifted and jeans unzipped. It was tantalizing but mostly terrifying. I was a curious teenage boy, but I would have preferred to explore on my own terms and at my own pace. The school was awash in scandals.

I reported none of this to my parents. Silence and shame—the two powerful jailers of my early life—had me imprisoned. My emotions were running wild, but those emotions remained locked up. I was painfully shy and hopelessly inexperienced. In my mind, I didn't stack up to my peers. At the same time, I longed to belong, to be "in."

My hormones were also running wild, but what to do about that? For all the talk of progressive learning, sex education was not part of the curriculum. My own education—if you can call it that—came from the pages of *Playboy*, *Hustler*, and *Oui*, the magazines I discovered my dad had hidden in the back of his closet. Those models—almost exclusively white women—became the objects of my fantasies. Those fantasies impacted the rest of my life. The one Black centerfold I remember seeing was in *Jet* magazine. That was also erotic. For a young teen, any half-naked woman was erotic. But given the lavish production values of their nude spreads, *Playboy* was the gold standard. And *Hustler*, because it was even more graphic. It was revelatory.

Masturbation felt good even as it felt bad. The climax was exciting even as it was disgraceful. It was a release and a relief—and also the cause of more guilt and shame.

During this time, my dad became even more critical. He was never happy with my report cards. His response to my grades was always, "You aren't really trying. Your study habits are atrocious. If you

don't improve, and improve quickly, you're bound to fail in life."
Even when my teachers thought I was bright enough to skip a grade,
Dad had no words of praise. As a result of my winning a couple of
spelling bees, I was given trophies. I proudly presented them to my
folks. Mom smiled. I don't remember Dad being particularly impressed.

I knew my mother cared for me, but she was caught up in her
own world, working hard on her degree. Affection was absent. Resentment was ever present. Back then if you had asked me what was
missing from my existence or simply what was wrong, I couldn't
have articulated the vast and sweeping sense of loneliness. But something was missing. I didn't know it then, but looking back it's easy to
pinpoint what that something was—I felt unloved. The search for
affection would haunt me for years to come.

14

SOFT AND WET

Music changed my life, but that change was long in coming. It took years to surrender myself, body and soul, to music's mystical powers. It wasn't that I resisted. I simply wasn't ready. I felt music with every fiber of my being, but I didn't understand its ability to transform.

For all my memories of Dad's putting me down, there are other memories—sweet memories—involving his love of music.

Dad liked jazz. Playing outside, I loved hearing those sounds coming from the house. The man was tight with money but dug music enough to buy a decent stereo.

He had taste. I can still picture him sitting in his easy chair, reading his *Wall Street Journal*, against the backdrop of an eclectic and seriously cool soundtrack. He played Ella Fitzgerald's versions of "Someone to Watch Over Me," Nancy Wilson's take on "Ode to Billie Joe," Sarah Vaughan's "I've Got a Crush on You," Diana Ross's "Love Hangover." At a young age, I appreciated the differences in their tones. Their voices touched me. Beyond his favorite singers, Dad had his favorite instrumentalists, guitarists Earl Klugh and Wes Montgomery, saxophonist Grover Washington Jr., pianist Bob James; groups, like Hiroshima; and fusion bands, like Weather Report.

Although I had begun to rebel against my father, I never rebelled against his music. I embraced his music even as I embraced music directed at my generation. I bought my first two singles in 1978: Funkadelic's "One Nation Under a Groove" and Prince's "Soft and Wet." I didn't know what either artist looked like and didn't care. Later I learned that "Soft and Wet" was Prince's first solo single and released on his twentieth birthday. When I heard it, I had just turned eleven. The lyrics—the reference to his sugarcane that he wants to lose inside his girlfriend—went over my head and straight to my feet. It made me want to move. I never thought twice about what was soft and what was wet. The jam was tight, the groove was right, and that's all that mattered.

Two years later Michael Jackson set the world on fire with *Off the Wall*. By then, barely a teen, I was convinced MJ was the second coming. Every cut on that album was superbad.

One Saturday afternoon, when the family was gone. I spent some time in my bedroom studying the blown-up photo on my wall of Kim Fields, who played Tootie on *The Facts of Life*. She was my first celebrity crush. From there I went to the living room and slipped on my dad's headphones and cranked up "Rock with You" so loud I thought my head would crack open. I wanted my head to crack open. I closed my eyes and danced like crazy. Naturally, I was trying to emulate Michael's moves. Because I was alone, I wasn't self-conscious. I had myself believing I could pop and lock with Michael's effortless grace. I was halfway to heaven when, in the middle of my frantic gyrations, I opened my eyes to see Dad standing there. How long had he been watching me? He stopped me in my tracks. He didn't laugh and he didn't smile. He didn't do anything but shake his head as if to say, "This boy has lost his mind." The party was over. I felt like a fool. But no matter; my connection to Michael's music only got stronger. When *Thriller* dropped, within a week I had it memorized.

Thanks to an iconic Detroit deejay, the Electrifying Mojo, I fell for the funk coming out of Minneapolis. Morris Day and the Time, Cherrelle, Alexander O'Neal, but especially Prince's unique brand of pop-soul R & B. I sensed a bravery in the way both he and Michael presented themselves to the world. They were not afraid of being different. Androgyny didn't frighten them. Musically, they were changing my world, opening my ears to slick syncopations and soaring melodies whose inspiration I feel to this day.

Though the influence of Michael and Prince was the most profound, I was deeply moved by music in other genres. I didn't think in terms of categories. And that's remained largely unchanged. To me, a great song is a great song. It doesn't matter if it's country, rock, jazz, classical, or blues. The groove is the groove and melody is king. I couldn't help but be intrigued by Simon and Garfunkel's "Bridge over Troubled Water." I was into Gordon Lightfoot, the Carpenters, the Captain & Tennille, the Bee Gees. I loved the Staples' "I'll Take You There," Rose Royce's "Car Wash," Cher's "Gypsys, Tramps and Thieves," Minnie Riperton's "Lovin' You," Bill Withers's warm "Lovely Day," and Bob Marley's deadly "I Shot the Sheriff." Not to mention Michael Franks's silky-smooth "Popsicle Toes."

I had my own musical moments in middle school that may have made the whole Michigan Institute experience worthwhile. I was in the ninth grade when a teacher named Greg Smith saw my interest in music and allowed me to poke at the piano. I kept playing the same three or four notes. I still didn't know about chords. But Mr. Smith did show me how to break down a song whose melody had haunted me — "Just My Imagination" by the Temptations. It was a dozen years old but still sounded new to me. It was complex. Patiently, Mr. Smith delineated its many parts. I'm not sure I took it all in, but I was fascinated. Before that, I had never considered the regimented structures that could produce a hit song.

There was one song, though, that I had flat-out ingested—George Benson's version of "On Broadway," a cover of an old Drifters hit from the early 1960s that had found new success in the late 1970s. I felt so good about my ability to render it right that one afternoon before class I started singing it a cappella. A few kids gathered around and urged me on. My first live performance. From then on, they kept requesting it. One time the teacher walked in while I was midchorus. She dug it too and let me sing it through. I can't call this an epiphany. I was far from envisioning a career for myself in music. It was just a nice moment, a boost when, in all other areas of my life, I was riddled with insecurity.

Which may be why I tied myself to the smartest kid in school, Bartow Thomas Jr. He was an extroverted, rough-and-tough football player type guy. He was brimming with confidence, which was probably why I became Robin to his Batman. Bartow gave me the cover I needed. I liked the role. I also liked the role of class clown. Richard Pryor was one of my favorite comedians. I could recite Bill Cosby's "The Chicken Heart That Ate New York" word for word. I thought I was a pretty funny dude. Despite the scandal and abuse, middle school wasn't all doom and gloom.

Hanging with cats like Bartow helped. Doing comedy bits, making people laugh, also seemed like an effective way to navigate my insecurities. But these moves were distractions. They were cover-ups. I was still shy. My shyness was rooted in confusion. Who was I? My dad saw me as damaged goods, an attitude I embraced.

When I left middle school to start Pontiac Northern High, I was desperate to sustain my sanity and, in doing so, found myself doing the most insane shit imaginable.

15

UP IN SMOKE

Even before I got to high school, I'd been stealing butts of Kool cigarettes out of my father's ashtrays and sneaking outside to smoke with my friends. When Dad caught me, he sat me down and made me smoke a whole pack. Which made me sick but didn't stop me from wanting to smoke. Smoking always interested me. As kids we would make our own cigarettes. We used strips of brown paper bag to roll up leaves. Not the best smoke in the world but it got the job done. Tobacco and leaves were one thing, but smoking weed was something altogether different.

Stacy, an older cat in the neighborhood, let me take a few hits off his joint as we walked to what would be my first day of high school. I liked being around Stacy because I had a crush on his younger sister Andrea, an affection that was never reciprocated. Andrea wasn't there on the morning that I lost my marijuana virginity. Good thing, because I don't know what I might have done. The weed turned me out, turned me upside down, threw me into a mental space I'd never experienced before. By the time I reached school, I was high as hell—flying. In art class, I was making strange-ass drawings that made no sense. I don't know if getting high made me happy. I do know that smoking that joint took me to an alternate reality. A reality much more tolerable than the one I had been living in. Later I'd use other substances to self-medicate, but in the beginning I was just a kid looking for whatever high I could get my hands on.

Thirteen is young to start high school. It happened because I'd skipped a grade back in middle school. I was small and skinny, and the world of Pontiac Northern was big and wide. I was overwhelmed. The enormity of the physical school, the enormity of the student body, the fact that you changed classes all the time, the phenomena of assemblies and school plays and pep rallies. Where did I belong in all this? Like a turtle, I hid inside my shell.

I have good recall, yet freshman year is blotted out of my brain. It may have something to do with the overwhelming sense of fear I felt. It was as if for the first time my academic performance really mattered. In middle school, I'm not sure they even gave grades. But at Pontiac Northern, I was always being tested. Because school was within walking distance, I ran home in a hot hurry. I liked getting home so I could space out.

Mom and I spaced out together. She stayed blitzed on beer while, with my bedroom window wide open to blow away the stink, I did my best to get off on a roach I'd found.

Mom had graduated from Wayne State and found a job at Detroit Bank and Trust in Birmingham, an affluent white suburb. She was in the management training program. That meant starting out as a teller. As the only Black employee in the bank, she fulfilled their equal opportunity mandate but was not made to feel welcome. The job didn't last long because Dad kept refusing to buy a second car, making transportation from Pontiac a nightmare. So, she went back to being a homemaker. She and Dad were always arguing. Yet he was the provider. Mom seemed to accept her circumstances but I could tell there was resentment building since Dad had stood in the way of Mom's ambition. But she did nothing about it—at least not yet. The dark mood of our household followed me when I went off to high school. Mom was tense. So was Dad. I can't speak for my sisters, but my tension was off the charts.

Some things helped, especially those rare visits from my grandmother. Katherine Owens, the woman I called Mother, would show up every once in a while, driving all the way from Nashville in her Buick Regal. Mom's mom never lost her affection for me. I loved her visits. Loved the attention she lavished on me.

The relationship between Mom and Mother was still strained. They did their best to tolerate one another. I still didn't know the reason for the strain and wasn't about to ask. While in Pontiac on one of her visits, Mother found a Pentecostal church where she could worship. Mom didn't join her. Neither did I. But Mother didn't mind. As usual, we stayed silent. Yet in spite of the unspoken feelings and underlying discord, at the end of Mother's visit, I was sad. It would be months, even years, before she returned.

Maurice and my dad's brother, Billy, were more regular visitors. Maurice came to visit every Thanksgiving, and Uncle Billy spent every Christmas with us and stayed through New Year's. I was happy to have them around. They brought a light and an energy that switched up the vibe in our heavy household.

———

At first, Dad seemed elated about my entering Pontiac Northern. He was even proud. He said that I was a big boy, that I was becoming a man. But with that pride came high expectations. To please him, I had to perform.

Rather than helping, the fact that I had skipped a grade actually made me more vulnerable. I wasn't sure I belonged in high school. After school, Mom and I watched television, our favorite pastime. *The Young and the Restless* for her, *The Three Stooges* for me. If only getting lost in fiction could have helped us forget our problems. My mother and I felt each other's sadness. We were both unhappy and didn't know how to convey what we felt. Expressing our feelings didn't even cross our minds.

TV was a strong focal point. It covered our silence. If I was caught acting up and Dad took away the TV, it felt like somebody had died. TV was my lifeline. I loved *The Jeffersons, Good Times,* and Flip Wilson dressed up as Geraldine. I loved *Soul Train*. Loved watching Rick James strutting out his "Super Freak." Loved hearing Chaka Khan blasting "What Cha' Gonna Do for Me." Loved Earth, Wind & Fire's "Let's Groove." I was fixated, and Dad was always quick to express his disdain.

School was Dad's fixation. Because he had excelled in school and because intellectualism was so important to him, he expected the same of me. I never met those expectations. Never came close. School was the thing that interested me least. At Pontiac Northern, it wasn't about academics; it was about football. Metropolitan Detroit was football crazy. The Pontiac Silverdome, a state-of-the-art stadium, had opened only a few years earlier. The Lions roared. The Pontiac Northern Huskies were idolized at pep rallies while the band blasted Queen's "Another One Bites the Dust." As those cute cheerleaders turned somersaults, I focused on their skimpy outfits. My hormones were in overdrive. I was as horny in high school as I was lonely. Having sex was an impossibility. I had to settle for stealing Dad's well-worn magazines for a quick study of each Playmate of the Month. As an undersized high school freshman, I had as much of a chance with the curvaceous cheerleaders as I did of playing linebacker for the Lions.

At school, the music room continued to call to me. I could sit at the Steinway piano for hours, striking notes and trying to create melodies. I joined the choir, but there were no public performances. No one telling me, "You have talent." Or, "You should keep singing." My job was to sell candy bars to raise money for the choir fund. Each bar cost a dollar. I found a way to pocket some of the proceeds. I got caught and was chewed out in a letter sent to my parents, which, of course, they never saw.

Mom, on the other hand, was always searching for another path. Our prospects for getting out of Pontiac and into a cooler neighborhood—nicer houses, better schools—were daunting. She never stopped bugging Dad. She wanted an upgrade for all of us. Being unapologetically cheap, Dad flatly refused. He placated her by driving us around on Sunday afternoons looking at for-sale homes he had no intention of purchasing.

One of Dad's fantasies was hitting the lottery. He had me write hundreds of white labels with his name and address to submit to an endless series of promotions that promised trips to Hawaii, new Chevy Impalas, or thousands of dollars in cash. He managed to win a few small household items over the years but not the big windfall he had his heart set on. At the same time, in what seemed a real-life miracle, Lady Luck did show up at our front door. Before her appearance, though, I received an even greater shock.

16

WHAT'S IN A NAME?

I had a bad habit of rifling through Dad's things. On one Saturday morning I opened the bottom drawer of his desk and something caught my eye. Underneath a couple of old business books and newspaper articles was a manila folder. Little did I know that its contents would leave an indelible mark on my life. It was my birth certificate.

The date was accurate, July 23, 1967, but my name was listed as Kim Owens—Owens was my mother's maiden name—and my father was listed as Jesse Nance Jr.

But I was Kim Hardy, wasn't I? Hadn't I always been Kim Hardy?

I kept looking at the lettering. Could it be a mistake? Could I be hallucinating? No. The date was right. The hospital was right. The facts were there in black and white. Yet I couldn't wrap my mind around one fact: Erick Hardy was not my father. Jesse Nance Jr. was.

You'd think I'd have run to Mom and started screaming, "*Who the hell is Jesse Nance Jr.? Why didn't you tell me your husband isn't my father? Why y'all lying to me? When were you going to tell me?"*

And yet, I didn't say a word. Not only did I not say a word then, I didn't mention it for another four years.

Because I had been going through my father's things, I knew how he'd play it. He'd chastise me for going through his things. He would turn my life-changing find into another example of my being a "dumb shit." I'd never hear the end of it.

I could have waited till Dad wasn't around and simply confronted my mom. But I didn't do that either. I didn't want to hurt her, and I knew bringing up this question would do just that. Besides, having this issue explode would undoubtedly add to the already bad vibes between my mother and the man I now knew was not my biological father.

I decided the only course of action was to take no action. The only solution was silence. Anything was better than dropping a bomb and watching what was left of our fragile domestic life go up in smoke.

Meanwhile my mind was a muddle. When we went for drives, I sat in the back of the car watching my father's hands on the steering wheel. I used to think my hands looked like his, but now I saw the difference. I remembered all those sweltering summers in West Palm Beach when someone would say, "You look just like your dad," or "You sound just like your dad," or "That's something your dad would do." I took those observations to heart, observations that, I now knew, were bullshit. I didn't, in fact, look or talk or walk or even think like my dad, because he wasn't my dad.

The realization that the story you've been told about yourself is a blatant lie is a hell of a thing to process. In fact, I didn't process it at all. I kept it buried inside and covered with shame, because, I reasoned rightly, the secrecy surrounding my birth was the result of shame. Someone—this Jesse Nance Jr., my Liz Owens—had done something too shameful to reveal.

17

LADY LUCK

In the summer of 1981, when Mom was thirty-one years old and I was about to turn fourteen, good fortune visited our family in spectacular fashion. It happened on a Sunday when Dad was too tired to go to the store. As a fervent coupon clipper and the guardian of the checkbook, he insisted on bargain hunting by himself. He liked coming home and letting us know the exact amount he'd saved with his coupons. It was unusual to see Mom do the shopping.

She went to our local Farmer Jack supermarket, picked up the items we needed, filled her basket, and presented her coupons to the cashier, then decided to buy a lottery ticket for a dollar. She didn't know much about lotteries. That was Dad's specialty. But when the High Score scratch-off showed five basketballs on top and she saw the number $25,000 beneath it, her heart started pounding. She didn't want to declare victory because of what had happened a year before. Dad had bought a lottery ticket he was convinced was worth

$10,000. After they celebrated, though, they discovered they had misread the card by three zeros. They'd won ten dollars, not ten thousand. This time Mom was extra cautious. She handed the card to the cashier and asked if seeing was believing.

"Honey," said the cashier, "you're looking at twenty-five thousand dollars' worth of mean green. Congratulations!" The cashier shouted it out across the store — "We got us a winner! We got us a winner!" — and suddenly Mom was a star. Everyone wanted to hug her, hoping her good luck would rub off. She drove home in a state of bliss, running into the house and yelling, "I won! I won!" Dad took the ticket and examined it for at least ten minutes. He was thinking about their earlier mistake. But the more he scrutinized it, the better it looked.

When the reality of the situation hit Dad, he cautioned Mom against letting anyone know. In the blink of an eye the world would come knocking on our door. But Mom already had one person in mind she had to tell. Her first and only call would be to the real estate agent. She was going to buy us a house.

———

The colonial-style home was on a well-manicured tree-lined street so clean-cut I felt like the Brady Bunch might be living next door. There were four bedrooms, two and a half baths, a finished basement, an attached garage, and a pretty yard. It was situated in Southfield, a suburb some fifteen miles north of downtown Detroit with a population of seventy thousand. This was by far the biggest change our family had undergone since moving from Nashville — even bigger, because our socioeconomic upgrade was so dramatic.

The house was cool, although its history, which was revealed long after we had moved in, was chilling. Its previous owner, Sol

"Good-Looking Solly" Shindel, had been bludgeoned to death with a fireplace poker and shot twice in the face right there in the living room. The newspaper called it a Mafia hit. Maybe that's why the selling price was well below market value.

———————

My identity crisis coincided with our move to Southfield. I was happy that Mom had won the lottery and was able to buy our first house. But I was furious with my father, who had always held himself up as a paragon of virtue. "Be true in everything you do and say." His usual spiel hit these points: You go to work. You do your job. You do it well. You advance. And your progress is based on your integrity.

Dad read widely and spoke of the men he admired—financiers, politicians, writers—whose greatest qualities were honesty and intelligence.

Well, if that was the case, my dad could not be counted among those men. He had not been honest with me. He had flat-out lied about being my father. And if I wasn't willing to confront him, I nonetheless had the tool—*his* tool—of passive aggression. I could be curt. When he spoke to me, I looked the other way. I expressed contempt by remaining quiet. If he asked me a question, I'd answer with a single word. *No. Yes. Maybe.* And that was it.

"What are you angry about?" he asked.

"Nothing," I lied.

I was angry about everything. Especially the fact that he wasn't my father.

Our living quarters were bigger. Our neighborhood was better. But I didn't feel bigger or better. I felt worse. It felt like we were the Beverly Hillbillies in the fancier social setting of Southfield. I still didn't have the shirts with the little polo player. I didn't even know what polo was.

"Kim done moved to Southfield," said one of my Pontiac friends. "Now he's eating French fries with a fork."

One of my early memories of our Southfield crib was one of those familial moments that were few and far between. Mom knew I loved comedy and let me sit in the living room when she and my father invited a group of friends over to watch Eddie Murphy's *Delirious* on cable. Even Dad, despite his best efforts, couldn't contain himself. Eddie was too damn funny for anyone to resist.

18

THE SOPHOMORE CHRONICLES

Leaving Pontiac, I entered Southfield High as a sophomore. It was predominantly white, with the Black minority consisting of students I saw as Cosby kids, privileged children of professionals. I'd faced a similar situation back in middle school at Michigan Institute for Child Development. The difference was that Michigan Institute was small while Southfield High was huge. For the next three years, I was lost.

While I attended Southfield High, smoking weed and drinking beer became everyday things. Sometimes before school, sometimes after. My dependency grew gradually but steadily. The more uncomfortable I became, the more out of place I felt, the more I got high.

Sometime early in my raggedy high school career, I lost my virginity. I had long dreamed about my first sexual encounter. The objects of my fantasies had been both Hugh Hefner's airbrushed white models and the Black chicks with fine figures walking through the hallways and the malls. The first woman to allow me in, though, was far from a model and wouldn't have been considered fine. She was, though, a friendly girl with a sweet personality. Her thick figure didn't bother me at all. I was more than willing. She seemed to be broken, like me, and also more than willing. Or maybe she just liked me. Either way, we were cool. It happened at school when the bell had rung and most of the students had filed into their classrooms. I wish I could tell you that we made love in a garden of pillows in front of a fireplace or on a king-size bed with silk sheets and scented candles. I wish I could tell you that words of affection were spoken, that we enjoyed prolonged and tender foreplay.

But the truth is that I had just finished smoking a joint and had somehow convinced her that a stall in the girls' bathroom was a suitable spot. I don't know what it was about me and bathroom stalls. We didn't make love. We fucked standing up. I think it's safe to assume she didn't enjoy it. I know I felt terrible about it. I felt guilty. Ashamed. That old terminology I'd been hearing for years—"the nasty"—fit the bill. I felt nasty. And the only way to relieve myself of this nasty guilt was to get as high as I possibly could and try to forget our sordid little episode.

There was no one to talk to about what had happened. Because I felt so bad about it, I wasn't about to boast to the boys. Besides, I wasn't a boaster. The few friends I had fit into one of two categories: outsiders or musicians.

As an outsider, romance didn't come naturally to me. When it came to girls, I didn't have any game. Sexual desire was one thing, but forging a real relationship was something else.

———

At fifteen, I fell hard for a Jewish girl named Rebecca whom I met at summer school. She lived only a few blocks away. Looking back, I can see that she was an archetype of the kind of woman that would enchant me for years to come. She was a beautiful brunette with long hair and a lovely olive complexion. She was smart. She was different. Her father wore a yarmulke, a skullcap showing his religious devotion.

Rebecca spoke softly; she spoke intelligently; she seemed intrigued by me. I was head-over-heels intrigued by her. We never had full-out sex, just a lot of making out in the back of her dad's station wagon. But I didn't mind. I wanted far more from her than sex. For the first time, I was infatuated. I dreamed of her day and night. When we walked together holding hands, an electric charge coursed through my body. For the first time, I experienced intimacy. Intimacy thrilled me. Intimacy changed the way I viewed the world. With intimacy, the world was wonderful. Without it, the world was unbearable. My feelings for Rebecca felt like genuine love.

But Rebecca and I didn't last long. It was more a dream than a season, but a dream that, throughout my life, I sought to rediscover and reclaim. I can't remember when or why we went our separate ways. Maybe it was the racial issue. Maybe she got tired of me. Either way, I was left lonely. This loneliness cut deep. I felt cut off from my sisters and my parents, who had sunk deeper into their individual bubbles. There was nowhere to run, nowhere to hide. So I decided to have another sip. Take another hit. And then turn to the one thing that offered heady excitement without the pain of a hangover: music.

19

MUSICAL SEEDS

Seeds planted deep inside. Seeds planted decades before my birth. Seeds from Africa spreading to Alabama, up through Tennessee, and straight into Detroit City. Beboppers, doo-woppers, scat-singing chicks, smooth-singing cats, crooners who calmed the restless soul of a troubled people. From the Saturday-night scramble to the Sunday-morning sanctity, it was all a part of me. It was my inheritance. I couldn't articulate it then. But without having the words to describe it, I could see those seeds were slowly starting to sprout.

I'm not sure when I became aware of perhaps the most potent seed. By the time I got to high school, Al Jarreau, who began as a jazz singer, had seamlessly moved to pop. "Mornin'," a joyful anthem, hit the top ten. What seemed like a whimsical lyric turned sacred when, at the bridge, he sang about touching the face of God.

I mention the man because he got inside my soul. Nat Cole was smooth. So were Sam Cooke and Marvin Gaye. All masters. But

Jarreau gave smoothness new meaning. He was both a scatter—a wordless improviser—and a full-throated crooner. He sang like an instrument. And he had mastered that instrument. His vocal flexibility was extraordinary. He told an interviewer that his two main influences were Johnny Mathis, the pop crooner, and Jon Hendricks, the jazz vocalese virtuoso. Al said that he sought to combine the two. It wasn't till years later that Al's *Heaven and Earth* album knocked me on my ass. I studied his every phrase.

Though the flexibility and uniqueness of Jarreau's voice could be intimidating, deep down I knew I had a voice of my own. "On Broadway" had proven that. But with my sense of self in the toilet, I felt like shit. I couldn't begin to acknowledge my talent, yet it was easy to spot the talent of others.

A classmate named Lori Thomas had crazy chops, sometimes sounding like Mahalia Jackson, other times like Sarah Vaughan. Another classmate, Doug McCollough, was the Stevie Wonder of Southfield High. At one of the school's talent shows, he and two of his friends turned out Michael Jackson's "Don't Stop 'Til You Get Enough" to the point where I slid down in my seat thinking, *Who the fuck am I to think that I can do this music thing?*

And yet . . .

In the music room I met Brian "Bean" O'Neal, a laid-back and extremely cool cat who was proficient at piano. He understood key changes. I didn't. He knew all about chords. I knew nothing. All I knew was that I loved Prince's "Do Me, Baby" and wanted to learn it on keyboard. The song fascinated me, both Prince's version and, later, the cover by Meli'sa Morgan. It was more than the sexed-up subject matter, although I dug the sexed-up subject matter. It was more than the grinding groove, although the grinding groove was good to me. It was the structure. What amazed me about "Do Me, Baby" was the fact that the song is based on just one chord progression. I wanted to break it down and see what made the whole thing tick. I couldn't do that alone. I needed Brian to show me.

I wasn't a quick study, but I was committed. I stayed at that keyboard for hours on end. I couldn't read a textbook for more than a few minutes, yet there I was, concentrating on the melodic structure of a song like a scientist in a lab. Was that really me, putting in an effort to learn something challenging? Yes, I did it. But then what did I do *with* it?

Nothing. My drinking and drug use worsened. I got to the point where I'd rather have been stoned than straight. I loved music, but I loved getting high more. Some people can combine those two loves, and for years I tried. But ultimately, I failed.

20

WE ARE THE WORLD

Because Mom was in full-blown addiction, she didn't see what was happening with me. She had fallen into depression. I've come to believe that depression is contagious. If the mood of a household is one of despair, that mood will surely impact everyone, especially someone as sensitive as me. As for her drinking, she remained in denial. A beer now and then, or a few every hour or two; what difference did that make? She was never a fall-down drunk. But, like me, she withdrew inside herself and away from her family. Once, against heavy odds, Mom had been ambitious enough to finish college and earn a degree. Yet she still didn't have a job or career. And maybe, just maybe, she would have found the courage to confront all this if she hadn't become pregnant in 1983. It happened when she was thirty-three, I was sixteen, Ericka was twelve, and Karen was eleven. During the pregnancy, she stopped drinking. But after Karmen was born in the winter of 1984, she went back to it.

Teenagers have lots of energy. I sure did. But in the eleventh grade, that energy took a nosedive. I withdrew from anything that smacked of positive action. My life was unraveling because of my misdeeds. Beer became my best friend because it was easy to get. I thought nothing of strolling into Rite Aid and strolling out with a case of Bud, the preferred brew in our household, without bothering to pay.

I couldn't see beyond my next high. I had a friend who, at sixteen, looked twenty-six, making it easy for him to cop from the party stores during lunch. We started doing speed, acid, and mescaline. At first it was exhilarating to be having these new, chemically induced experiences. But the negative energy remained the same. I tried a co-op plan offered by school that let me work and study. I found a job at a shoe store. It was close enough to walk to from my house. On its face, it seemed like the right move. But as it turned out, the place was a drug-crazed scene led by a corrupt manager who was cooking up coke down in the stockroom. It was my introduction to freebasing, the more elegant and labor-intensive form of smoking crack cocaine.

At home, the vitriol between me and Dad only escalated. I felt he was a fraud, and my unwillingness to confront him, to once and for all scream out, *"You ain't my daddy! You ain't ever been my daddy! And you won't ever be my daddy!"* only fueled the fire.

He was pissed at me for making poor grades and shirking my responsibilities. I was pissed at him for living a lie. The flame might have once been low, but now it was white-hot. One night the pot boiled over. In all of our fights and arguments I had always kept my mouth shut. I had never talked back. Then came the moment when for the umpteenth time he called me a "dumb shit" and I blew up. I let him have it. No doubt I was drunk, and no doubt the booze made me brave. I laid into him, cursing and screaming and calling him a tyrant. It all came back to me. His coldness. His callousness. How he had abandoned me summer after summer by shipping me off to Florida. How he never had a kind or encouraging word. How he made me feel worthless. "This is your fault!" I screamed at my dad. "Your fuckin' fault! Your fuckin' rules! Your fuckin' fake-ass bullshit!" And yet, in this wild tirade, I still didn't reveal the fact that I knew he wasn't even my real father.

I didn't have to. My combative words were enough to set him off. He grabbed me by the neck and dragged me up the stairs. I was choking and kicking at him at the same time. Mom and my sisters were screaming. Only the intervention of Dad's brother, visiting for the holidays, kept things from turning tragic. Uncle Billy managed to separate us, but after that day our relationship took a permanent downward turn.

The violent confrontation frightened Mom, but she didn't intervene. She was an alcoholic, yet she had managed to tap into her ambition. That ambition had led her to a part-time job at the Empire of America bank. She was soon promoted from teller to paralegal. She was getting somewhere.

I was getting nowhere. My last year of high school was the worst. My folks didn't know how bad it was because I kept destroying my report cards. It got to where they even stopped asking how I was doing in school. They knew. I skipped more classes than I attended. When it came time for graduation, I was allowed to walk across the stage, but only to be handed a blank certificate. My mother knew. My father didn't. He assumed that I had actually graduated.

The graduation ceremony was as empty as my certificate, except for one moment. The choir assembled to sing "We Are the World." I was tapped to sing Tina Turner's line—"We're all a part of God's great big family"—which she had sung after James Ingram and before Billy Joel. A small part, but I gave it all I had. The audience reacted with shouts of encouragement. It'd be nice to report that I took that encouragement as an altar call. I'd love to tell you that it became an instance where I could see that, yes, I had talent that required cultivation and care, and from that point forward, I put my shoulder to the wheel.

But I didn't. At the high school graduation party, I saw my friend Nick, the son of a Greek tool-and-die magnate, who lived on the other side of town. Nick was cool. We liked hanging out and chopping it up while cruising in his Camaro IROC-Z. He probably could have gotten me a job at his father's firm, but I never asked. After a few drinks, Nick said he was taking off.

"Where you going, man?" I asked.

"I've had enough."

Those words stuck with me. What did he mean by *I've had enough*? I hadn't had enough, not enough beer, not enough Four Roses. I'd stay until the very last drop was drunk and then I'd go looking for more to drink.

There would never be enough.

21

THIS CONVERSATION
NEVER HAPPENED

When I turned eighteen in 1985, I decided to apply for a driver's license using the name on my birth certificate—Kim Owens. That was a major decision. Until then I had always been Kim Hardy. I can't say why I chose that moment. Maybe it was my first declaration of independence. If so, the declaration was forthright, but the independence was not. I was still heavily dependent on staying high.

I was in the house, filling out the application at the dining room table. Dad wasn't around. Mom came over and noticed what I was doing. For the first time since I had discovered the truth years earlier, the issue was raised.

"Why are you calling yourself Kim Owens?" she asked.

"Because that's the name on my birth certificate. They won't give me a license without my birth certificate."

There was a long pregnant silence. She sighed. I looked away. The silence lingered. The silence went on forever.

Finally, she said, "Are there any questions you'd like to ask me?"

I had a million questions. Even still, I said no.

"So, you're okay with all this, Kim?"

"Yeah, I'm cool."

And that was it. We never had a discussion. Never came close to a conversation. Mom simply accepted the fact that I didn't want to know. I accepted the fact that she didn't want to explain. For all the discomfort associated with silence, we both found it to be the easier, softer way.

I was more comfortable drinking than talking. Although it was obvious, I didn't use the term that directly applied to my condition:

I was an alcoholic.

Mom didn't call herself an alcoholic until she hit rock bottom. That happened when I was out on the streets while she was trying to keep her job at the bank. She put up a good front. And then came the day of reckoning. She'd been off work for a couple of weeks to replenish her energy. When she returned to the bank, her desk was piled high with papers. Documents were scattered everywhere. Dozens of notes, dozens of phone calls to return, a thousand details. She took one look and broke down. Right there at Empire of America, with customers, tellers, and executives watching, she burst into tears and collapsed. She was driven to the hospital. The initial exam showed nothing was wrong with her physically. But the doctor had the good sense to see that everything was wrong with her emotionally. When she admitted her drinking problem, he recommended rehab. She entered a twenty-one-day treatment facility and was introduced to a twelve-step program. That saved her life. Meanwhile, I was running the streets, completely unaware of what was happening with her.

22

"OUT!"

My father shouted and pointed to the door.

"Out!"

We were at a flashpoint. I'd come home blasted for the umpteenth time. But this time my father wasn't letting me back in. I wanted to speak to my mom.

"She doesn't want to talk to you. She's in the family room resting and doesn't want to be disturbed." He stopped me before I could say another word. "These are her orders," he said. "Your mother doesn't want to see you. She's fragile. Having you around is only going to make things worse. Disappear."

I had come home late many times before to find myself locked out. I would throw pebbles at my sisters' bedroom window so Ericka would come down and let me in. She was always sympathetic and helped me out when she could. But when Mom learned what Ericka was doing, she threatened to throw her out as well. Mom didn't play.

Now Mom wasn't talking and Dad was in charge. She was not long out of rehab, a fact that Dad wasn't about to broadcast. I wasn't sure if the secrecy stemmed from his attempting to protect our family's privacy or if he was simply ashamed his wife was an alcoholic. Either way, I was out.

For the next few years, my mother and I had little contact. Physically, we saw each other from time to time. I could always call and she'd always listen. But we still had little to say. She sensed—and rightly so—that all I wanted to do was get high. I wasn't about to listen to anybody. I knew she'd found a new gig and was making good money. I knew she was working the steps. I knew she had even found a chilled-out church where recovery groups met every hour on the hour. I knew her spirit was being renewed. From afar, I sensed that she was growing. I always had my eye on my mother. Always have and always will. But back in 1988 and 1989, as her story took a turn for the better, mine took a turn for the worse.

Mom and Dad on their wedding day.

Me at four years old at our Nashville apartment.

First grade.

An early high school photo.

Sitting at the kids' table. Left to right: my sister Karen, me, and sister Ericka.

Thanksgiving dinner. Left to right: me, Mom, and sister Ericka.

Snow day with my sister Ericka and our infamous Plymouth Satellite.

Sam Donahoo,
Bob, and me (1987).

In the studio at the
keyboard (late 1980s).

Me and Lori Thomas
recording a duet in
Wyandotte, Michigan.

The men of
The Gospel Truth.
Left to right:
me, Yogi Brock,
Michael Brock,
Ralph Mitchell,
Chris McKee.

Half Past 3 in Detroit. Left to right:
Dave McMurray, me, Fred Robinson,
and Quentin Baxter.

My sister Karen
and her son, Justin.

Me and Troi on a Disney cruise.

Troi and Mom in D.C.

Ten-year-old
Alexandria (Alex).

Left: Walking my sister Karmen down the aisle (September 2007). *Dorian Gonzalez*

Below: My sister Karmen's wedding in 2007. In the back row is Mom, Aunt Tina, Karmen, Fabian, Aunt Ruth, Aunt Prince. Front row: Aunt Katherine, Mother, Cousin Lindsey. *Dorian Gonzalez*

My grandmother, Maurice Hardy.

Laylah about to swim with the dolphins.

Left: Troi and Laylah.

Below: Me and Troi on her graduation day.

Me and Erica (2018). *Cybelle Codish*

Two-year-old Kristoffer.

Mr. and Mrs. Owens at home, 2018. *Cybelle Codish*

Left to right: Izzy, Kristoffer, Trinity, and Erica at home, 2022. *Cybelle Codish*

23

CURSE OF THE DOWNWARD SPIRAL

Just when you think you're all the way down, you've got a helluva lot further to fall."

I didn't want to hear those words. Didn't want to believe them. They came out of the mouth of an old man who was sharing a nasty bottle of wine with me. We were sitting out in a deserted park next to an abandoned factory. It was the middle of the day. I had just turned nineteen. I was sure he was sixty. It turned out he was thirty. I should have seen my future in his face. But all I saw was the fact that he had finished off the bottle and left nothing for me.

I moved on.

After Dad kicked me out, my main mission—the one thing that I thought of first every morning—was figuring out where I was going to spend the night. I'd left the house with a pillowcase stuffed with a pair of underwear, socks, a T-shirt, and a toothbrush. That first day

I hid it in the yard of the Rosens, our neighbors across the street. I didn't want to be someone walking around holding a pillowcase. I also didn't want to be someone who was sober. That meant heading over to CVS. On the way, I searched the sidewalk for cigarette butts. I had no pride about smoking cigarette butts. I dug them out of ashtrays and garbage cans. At the drugstore, I slipped a bottle of nasty wine inside my shirt, headed to the train tracks, and downed it in no time. A warm rush washed over me. It was all about that warm rush. I lived for it.

———————

A little later I met my boys, outliers like me, at the Clock Restaurant. By then I'd stolen and consumed a second bottle of wine. They put up with me, I suppose, because they thought I was cool. Even in my down-and-out state, I managed to keep some semblance of cool. I actually wore my hair in a perm. I walked with a little swag. I talked shit, even if my talking was a little slurred. And if I nodded out at the table, as I tended to do, and the manager came by and told my friends, "Tell your boy he can't flop here," they poked me awake. I'd smile as if nothing were wrong.

One of them would let me slip into his house and crash on the porch or in the basement. But before that, we'd drink Colt 45 or smoke weed to take off the edge.

The next day, more of the same. Wine, butts, and weed. I might wander over to a Citgo gas station where I used to work as a cashier and hang out with my friend Desmond, who'd been hired to take my place. One night, before he went outside to help a customer, I watched him put an envelope with the day's receipts into a drop box. When the envelope didn't fall all the way into the box, I was able to fish it out with a coat hanger and steal the money. I was a thief, a booster, and, at least in my conscious mind, had no compunction. God only knows the guilt that was building up in my head.

Even during these down days, I hadn't given up on music. And my high school friend Brian O'Neal hadn't given up on me. Along with Sam, the same Sam who'd let me sleep in the crawl space under his basement stairs, we formed a group called Wild Pair. Brian was on keys, while Sam and I worked on lyrics. I did the singing and most of the writing. The songs were terrible. The signature song, "Wild Pair," had lines like, "I'd rather spend the night with you . . . I know that you care . . . we're such a wild pair . . ."

But we were too young and dumb to know how terrible most of our songs were. We cut them on a primitive four-track sitting up on a milk crate and were convinced they deserved something better. We wanted to get into a real studio and make a real record. There was just one problem. We were broke.

That prompted me and Sam to devise a financial plan. Unfortunately, the plan was criminal. One night we had seen the manager of a retail store out in a distant suburb make his nightly deposit. How hard would it be to hold him up? The white dude was portly, middle-aged, and hardly intimidating. It'd be easy.

Sam had a car and found a mask. He'd do the driving and I'd handle the rest. What about a gun? He found one that didn't have bullets. That was fine with me. I could build up the nerve to do the heist but wasn't about to shoot anyone.

I say I'd built up the nerve, but that's an exaggeration. I was nervous as hell. Driving over there, I almost bailed. I almost shit my pants. But my stupidity overwhelmed my common sense. We parked across the street from the store, and at closing time—seven p.m. on the dot—the man locked up with a bag of money in hand. I looked in every direction and saw that the street was empty. I put on my mask and got out of the car. Sam nodded approvingly.

I slowly approached the man. My hands were shaking. He turned and looked at me. My mask said it all. I didn't even have to show him the empty gun. When he hesitated to turn over the loot, I was prepared to give up and run back to the car. But his hesitation lasted only a few seconds. He too was scared, and without saying a word, he handed me the bag. That was it.

With Sam at the wheel, I opened the bag and saw a bunch of checks and about seven thousand dollars in cash. We destroyed the checks and used the cash to book our first session at a recording studio.

I was obviously not in a decent headspace at the time. I was drunk and scared to death. What's even worse, I had frightened this poor guy in ways I couldn't possibly imagine. He could have had a heart attack. Stealing was one thing, but armed robbery was another. I told myself it wasn't *armed* robbery because the gun wasn't loaded. But if I'd been caught, what judge would have accepted that as a defense? I guzzled a forty-ounce of Colt 45, thirsting for oblivion.

24

HITTING BOTTOM

We found a good studio downriver in Wyandotte with far superior recording equipment. We went from recording on four tracks to recording on sixteen. The engineer acted as a producer, allowing us to layer instruments and vocals in ways we'd never done before. Hearing my voice reverberate in that professional setting was thrilling. I was high on weed, cocaine, wine, and music.

While they were retooling some technical stuff, I took a break to walk outside and sit on a small rocky cliff overlooking the Detroit River. While I took a toke off a half-smoked joint I'd found in a studio ashtray, I looked around me. Gulls were in flight. I could hear waves slapping against the rocks. In that moment, I felt like I was going somewhere. Music was finally taking me where I wanted to go. I was no longer just drifting through a life of alcohol, drugs, depression, and crime. I was becoming a singer, a songwriter, a recording artist.

I was living at Brian's when we moved our recording to Sound Suite Studios in Detroit proper. That's where I met David McMurray, a saxophonist who was recording with the funk group Was (Not Was), and his wife, Garzelle, who worked for the studio. Dave was a super-talented musician, adept at all the genres. We struck up a friendship, but that didn't save me from wreaking havoc on the place. I stole Richards Wild Irish Rose from the liquor store next door and stayed smashed. I got so crazy that I pulled a knife on another band that was recording. I can't remember why. But I can remember Mike Grace, the studio owner, trying to curb my craziness. I put my hand in my jacket as if I had a gun, pointing my finger at him. That scared Mike. Who, I later found out, had a real gun. He actually thought he was going to have to kill me that night. Violence was averted, but, in no uncertain terms, I was barred from the studio.

This whole musical operation was a farce. The engineer/producer convinced us to sign a deal. We thought we were on our way, but the alcohol-and-cocaine-fueled scene deceived us. We deceived ourselves. Hype ruled the day, and when push came to shove, we realized the truth: we'd spent all our money. And our music wasn't going anywhere.

If I had been depressed before, I was doubly depressed now.

After parting ways with Brian, I ended up back in Southfield. I was back to stumbling through my days until I begged, borrowed, or stole enough money to sit at the counter at White Castle eating four burgers for a buck. I caught the bus to Pontiac, where, as a last resort, I checked into a Salvation Army shelter. They gave me a cot to sleep on and a job in the kitchen that lasted only long enough for me to find a bottle of almond extract with a label that said it was 83 percent alcohol. Me and one of my bunkies were in the pantry mixing it with red Kool-Aid. When they found me passed out, they gave me the boot.

I avoided central Detroit because it seemed too hard-core. In my mind central Detroit was for heroin addicts and crackheads. If you can believe it, I made a distinction between my condition and what I saw as the far more degenerate condition of those poor souls strung out on heroin and crack. I guess I saw myself as being in a higher circle of hell.

Besides, I knew Southfield like the back of my hand. I knew which Rite Aids and liquor stores were easier to steal from. I knew that the telemarketing firm where I'd once worked part-time had a clean men's room on the ground floor I could nod off in if I needed to.

I went back to couch-surfing from one friend's house to another. The circle of friends, though, got smaller, until there were nights when I wound up sleeping under a tree in a public park. The next thing I knew, someone was tapping me on the shoulder. The sun half blinded me, but I could see it was a little kid. Wearing a backpack, he was on his way to school. He couldn't have been older than ten.

"You okay, mister?" he asked.

"I'm fine," I lied.

"I thought you might be dead. I've never seen a dead guy before."

"No, I'm alive."

"Well, I'm glad you're not dead. But why are you sleeping in the park? Don't you have a bed at home?"

I assured him that I had a bed and a home. I thanked him for caring and watched him go on his way.

I thought of myself as a child. I remembered when we'd first moved to Pontiac. Back then, things were looking up. Mom was pregnant. Dad had a new job. I was innocent. Nothing heavy had happened. Or had it? Had I already felt the tension between my parents? Was I feeling unwanted by my father? Was there ever a point in my childhood when I could call myself carefree?

These early morning thoughts got me nowhere. I just wanted to drink it all away.

Staying stoned in Southfield reached the point of diminishing returns. My cool, my perm, my swag—everything was coming undone. I had become too unpresentable for even loyal friends to let me in. I had to go looking for shelters. I had to leave the seemingly safe city of Southfield and go exactly where I didn't want to go. For all my determination to avoid hard-core Detroit, that's where I wound up.

One night I found myself walking by the Detroit River where a few homeless men and women had built fires and makeshift tents. Some covered themselves with old newspapers. I passed by a trash can overflowing with filthy garbage. I became that person who roots through refuse in the hopes of finding something, anything. I found a nasty old blanket. I wrapped it around my shoulders and sat on the ground. I could see Canada just across the river. The lights on the foreign shore twinkled like jewels. I looked at the Ambassador Bridge, which linked the two countries. Cars traveled in both directions. I had no direction. I thought of other people my age, others I'd known, others who were married with decent jobs and decent lives. I thought of the time I'd spent watching Robin Leach's *Lifestyles of the Rich and Famous* and chuckled to myself. I had fantasized about such lifestyles. Yet here I was, homeless and trying to keep warm with this tattered blanket. The can of King Cobra I was nursing and the loose change in my pocket represented everything I owned.

The Detroit of the late 1980s/early 1990s was in ruins, a city that reflected my own ruin. It had once been an industrial dynamo, a place where Blacks fleeing the rural South had found decent wages in the mighty plants built by GM, Chrysler, and Ford. Those days were long gone. Civil unrest, rough economic downshifts, and a plague brought on by crack were all disastrous contributors to the city's decay. White flight had stripped the urban center of its once-vibrant commercial and cultural life, leaving behind boarded-up buildings. Major institutions of learning—elementary, middle, and high schools—had been deserted and left to rot. The rows of ruined houses went on for miles and miles. Many were for sale for $100 or less.

Like Detroit's downfall, my own deterioration was fast-moving. Within weeks, I wound up in the Oakland County Jail for some infraction I can't remember. When I got out, I was told about another Salvation Army in Detroit. It was nicknamed the Sally and was located on Fort Street next to the main post office. For some strange reason I was nervous as hell walking into that place. Simply put, I felt like a loser. I had just entered my early twenties, but it seemed my life was over before it had begun.

25

A BEGINNING

Our lives begin to end the day we become silent
about things that matter.

—MARTIN LUTHER KING JR.

The first person I saw at the Sally was an older brother who looked
down at my prison-issued flip-flops, chuckled to himself, and said,
"You a long way from home, ain't you?" I couldn't help but laugh.
His comic relief was medicine to my soul.

The Sally was a big facility that housed about 150 men. I slept
in a dorm, a large room with a half-dozen beds and a common bathroom. The experience was humbling. And it wasn't as though I was
looking to be humbled. It came with the territory, and besides, I
didn't have a ton of options. It was the Sally or the streets.

One of the first brothers I met in the dorm was only a few years older than me and he was sober. This cat was always talking about the future. He talked about going back to school. Getting a job. Eventually moving out and moving on. He was always upbeat. I liked his energy, but at the same time, he got on my nerves. I was jealous of his motivation and positive outlook on life.

"Nothing to it but to do it," he said.

"Do what?" I asked.

"Go to a meeting." I'd been hearing about recovery groups from everyone, including my mother. But a recovery group seemed like too much work.

"Go to a meeting," the brother repeated.

The last thing I wanted to do was go to a twelve-step meeting. But I was envious enough of this dude to do just that—I followed him to a meeting. I wanted what he had, and if going to a meeting was the only way to get it, then damn it, I was going to a meeting.

———————

I walked in feeling like a deer in headlights. My first instinct was to run back out the door. But where would I go? More important, how long was I going to keep running? I had tried everything I knew, which wasn't much, to right the ship of my life. If my best thinking was only good enough to earn me a bed at the Salvation Army and a seat at a twelve-step table, what difference would it make if I left? Despite my reservations, I convinced myself to stay and sat down at a table.

I was terrified of being called upon to speak. I had never been in a room full of people who openly and candidly talked about their feelings. Though I obviously had a world of my own feelings bottled up inside, I wasn't about to uncork that bottle in a room full of strangers. I wasn't about to say a word.

Thankfully, I wasn't required to speak; I could just sit there and say nothing. Which was just what I did. And while I can't say I was comfortable at the initial meeting, I was intrigued. Strangers were speaking freely. Folks were spilling their guts about how they loved drinking and drugging; how they couldn't stop drinking and drugging; how drinking and drugging had ripped their lives apart; how some had gone over the precipice of insanity. One guy said he hated being there and hated the program. Another said he loved being there and loved the program. Someone else talked about his problems with his father. In a weird way, I related to everyone. The guideline against "cross talk" helped. That meant you couldn't respond to anyone. Everyone got to say whatever they had to say without worrying about a response. Responses were not the point. The point was to express feelings. Without judgment or reprimand.

For a non-speaker like me, this was a huge revelation. It was, in fact, one of the great revelations of my life.

I did not leave the meeting a believer. I still wanted to snuff out the dark feelings I harbored about myself with alcohol and drugs. But I realize now, as I didn't then, that simply going to the meeting confirmed a decision I had made. I had chosen life over death.

Yet weeks went by and I still didn't open my mouth. No one seemed to notice, or if they did, they didn't seem to care. Except for one guy. He said he'd seen me coming to all these meetings and wanted to know who I was. He wanted to know my story. I didn't know whether to be flattered or afraid. I didn't even think I had a story. Stories were things you read about in books. Stories were important. My sense of self was so low that I didn't think I was important enough to have a story. The only story I had was too shameful to rehash openly.

This cat, though, was aggressive. He kept pushing me. Somehow he knew I had something inside that needed to get out. He understood that you can go to meetings and not participate for only so long. My sole response to his prompting was to tell him I had nothing to say.

"Say something. Say anything."

At the next meeting I attended, he made it a point to sit next to me. When it came time for sharing, he gave me the kind of eagle-eyed look I couldn't ignore. Finally, I raised my hand.

The first words were relatively easy. I gave my name and said why I was there.

But what would come next?

"I'm not the talking type, so I'll just say that drinking and drugging has been messing me up for a long time."

Then silence.

Then applause.

The applause made me feel good.

And as the days went by, like a baby taking his first steps, I actually began to share.

I'd say things like, "I'm afraid of sharing because I'm afraid of looking bad. I hate looking bad."

Or, "I don't want to admit how ashamed I feel. I'm even ashamed of being ashamed. I've done so many stupid things I can't remember them all."

Or, "I'm only talking because you expect me to. I'd rather not say a word. I'd rather hide in the back of the room and pretend everything is fine."

Or, "I'm searching for something to say, but I don't know what that something is."

26

FEARLESS AND MORAL

The twelve-step program was the first time in my life when I was consciously aware that I was searching for something. I was searching for a way to better myself. Searching for a way to stop the hemorrhaging, the bleeding out of my life into this bottomless pit of despair.

My attempts at making music with Wild Pair weren't really a search for musical excellence. Sure, I was trying. The seeds of ambition had been planted. But I was too stoned to understand what searching was all about. I wanted a record deal, but my attempts to get one up until that point had been half-assed. I lacked the judgment to distinguish between the people wanting to help me and those wanting to exploit me.

The twelve-step paradigm rested on a belief in a higher power. That presented another search. Who was that higher power? What did it mean to put faith in that power?

Early into the program, I realized I wouldn't figure much out by myself, but answers could come from listening to other people.

For example, one dude said he considered himself an atheist so he couldn't see himself leaning on "God." And then he heard that a positive loving force—a higher power—could be anything outside himself. It could be the meetings. It could be long walks through nature. It could be anything that would rid us of the idea we could stop drinking on our own. We had to start somewhere.

I related to a sister who talked about having no willpower and no discipline. That was me. All my life, my dad had said so. But then she switched it up and saw that lack of willpower in a different way. Willpower, she said, is a myth. It's all about being willing. Being willing to listen, willing to ask for guidance, willing to learn.

Another brother talked about humility.

"In thinking I could wrestle this addiction monster to the ground," he said, "I was arrogant. I lacked humility. When I got humble enough to admit that the addiction was too strong to take on alone, things started to change."

A brother with long-term sobriety said, "I started out hating my addiction. I wanted to destroy it. But someone said the more I hate it, the more powerful it grows. Yet how I could I *not* hate it? My sponsor helped me see understanding my addiction was the better approach. I needed to offer compassion to the part of myself that craved alcohol and drugs. It was all a part of my humanity. And if you admit that you can't manage that part—the part that keeps you self-medicating your life away—you take pressure off yourself and turn elsewhere for support."

Yes, I thought, I can't manage that part of myself. Yes, it's a relief to hear talk like that. But isn't the whole point to manage your life so your life doesn't fall apart?

Getting control over my life meant admitting that I had no control over my life. Being powerless over my addiction meant admitting I had to seek help.

The bottom line was: submit to something you don't completely understand but, in your heart, you trust. The trust comes from seeing sincere strangers demonstrate their own journey to free themselves of negative forces that have been destroying their lives.

The search, as it turned out, was not a formal study. It didn't require research. It meant listening. For example, when someone said, "You're only as sick as your secrets," I thought my heart would bust out of my chest. *Secrets!* How many secrets had I been living with?

My mother had secrets. Her mother had secrets. I had secrets. Over generations, those secrets had been silenced, hidden, buried deep in the soil of our family history. Maybe I'd never know all those secrets. But I certainly knew mine.

My low self-esteem—actually my *no* self-esteem—had been fueled by secretive behavior. Little by little, in meeting after meeting, I let the secrets out. I spoke candidly about what I had done. Stealing, lying, and manipulating to get what I wanted.

If I had an "aha" moment in recovery, it had to do with the realization that my insane behavior was not exclusive to me. For example, my blackout episodes had terrified me. To learn others had experienced the same terror was comforting. Unexpectedly, I was in a room with people who had lived through what I had lived through. I was not alone. Beyond the bonding, I was told that there was a solution. This destructive thing could be fixed. I was given tools to transform my life. What a relief! Because we spoke the same language, I could relate to everyone. Whether it was a CEO of a Fortune 500 company or some guy who last week had been eating out of garbage cans, we were equals. I finally felt settled in a place filled with optimism and goodwill.

Now that I was through running, the real work could begin. The recovery process was simple. Trust God. Clean house. Help others. But it would not be easy. At times it would uncomfortable, intimidating, and painful. There's an adage I love that says, "Pain is mandatory, suffering is optional." I could accept the fact that, drunk or sober, there was no way to escape the pain of my life. The only way out was through. So, if I had to hurt anyway, I decided I might as well do it sober and walk into my destiny.

27

BORN AGAIN

July 23, 1990.

In addition to being my twenty-third birthday, it also marks the birth of my sobriety. Ever since that day, I've been free of mind-altering substances. No booze, beer, wine, weed, coke, crack—nothing. I've suffered no slips. I say that not arrogantly but factually. I don't believe I have conquered my addictions. My ongoing sobriety depends on daily spiritual maintenance. That means prayer, meditation, and reaching out to help others.

I can't go on cruise control, can't stop engaging in fellowship with my brothers and sisters in recovery, can't stop centering myself every morning in the recognition of God's hand on my life.

Getting sober did not mean instant success. But it did mean that I got to live. I didn't have to die young in a drunken stupor. I didn't have to spend the rest of my life in jail for killing someone while driving under the influence. I got to live.

Months ticked by. Ever so gradually, I felt my heart expanding. I heard myself opening up. I was telling strangers things I had never told myself. I was putting words to feelings that, until then, had never been given a voice. At the same time there were other voices, negative voices. They were relentless. *Once a drunk, always a drunk. You're a loser and always will be. All this sharing is getting you nowhere.* They spoke with authority. They pointed to the incontrovertible evidence that I had managed to do absolutely nothing with my life. They were ruthless and incessant. Their goal, I began to realize, was to bring me down. They wanted me dead.

Men and women with long-term sobriety taught me that acknowledging and expressing this internal dialogue was one way to reduce the power it seemed to have over me. Expressing it without judgment. Expressing it with the realization that, in one form or another, it will always be there. Eventually, we would learn to coexist.

On many days, I said I felt hopeless. On other days, I expressed my gratitude. On all days, I listened to others and allowed their stories to become part of my story. And by speaking, I allowed my story to become part of theirs.

It felt good to tell another human being exactly what was going on with me. The healing was in simply being able to sit down and talk to someone. I dealt with negative feelings by exposing them to daylight. Almost always, that exposure cut those negative feelings in half.

It took months to move up the Salvation Army food chain to where, instead of living in a dorm with six beds, I shared a room with just one other person. Meanwhile, everyone worked. My job was to ride shotgun on a truck that traveled around the city after midnight picking up donations—old clothes or canned food—from Salvation Army drop boxes and hauling them back downtown.

I didn't mind. I liked seeing deserted city streets at two a.m. I even began liking the fact that, rather than being drunk, I was a sober man doing honest work. I had purpose. I began noticing things I had not noticed before. If it snowed, I took in the beauty of buildings covered in white. Rain gave a romantic sheen to the city's landmarks: the moon shining down on the Detroit River; the ornate skyscraper on West Grand Boulevard that once served as General Motors' headquarters; farther down West Grand, Hitsville, USA, the Motown bungalow, which made me think of Smokey and Stevie and Marvin, the great masters who had long ago left the city, and in Marvin's case, left the planet; the Fox Theatre on Woodward Avenue, where they all performed. If the night was clear, I'd look at the stars in the sky. During my blurry and blacked-out addiction, I never noticed anything.

I was making progress while also trying to make up for lost time. I didn't consider myself brilliant, but I always knew God had blessed me with a good mind. It was ridiculous for me to not have finished high school. I wanted to set that right. That was the first benefit of sobriety: understanding the necessity of finishing what you start.

During this period there was a warrant out for my arrest. Before getting sober, I had been caught stealing a tall can of Miller Light from a Rite Aid in Royal Oak. I had gone to jail for a night but was released the following morning. My sentence, though, was pending. On a rainy Thursday morning, I caught a bus from the Salvation Army in downtown Detroit to the Royal Oak courtroom, where I faced a judge. I was terrified, but I was also prepared. When he asked me to speak, I explained that when I stole the beer I was feeding an addiction.

"That's not an excuse; my addiction is why I'm standing here."

I also explained that I was active in recovery. Fortunately, he gave me probation. On the bus back to the Salvation Army, I felt grateful for what the program had taught me: There are problems, but problems are not insurmountable. In all things, trust God.

With my newfound clarity I realized I desperately wanted to get my high school diploma. That required another bus ride from downtown to an adult education center in Oak Park every morning. Over a year's time, I took the required courses needed for my degree. Even after working midnights on the truck, I didn't mind the routine. The routine gave me structure. Go to a meeting, work on the truck, go to school. It was classic Detroit hustle. It was a grind. I found my groove in that grind and kept moving forward.

There were awkward moments. One of the administrators at the center was a woman who had been my classmate at Southfield High School. She had graduated and gone to college to become a professional educator. Here I was, age twenty-four, still trying to get my high school diploma.

She wasn't dismissive of me. She was simply curious.

"What happened to you, Kim?"

"I got sidetracked," was all I could say.

My new sense of responsibility didn't go unnoticed. I got promoted. I became the intake counselor at the Sally. It wasn't a paid position. Nor was it actual counseling. I was seated at a desk helping people who wanted to be admitted to the Adult Rehabilitation Center. That meant doing more of what I had learned to do at the meetings: listening. It required scrutiny. Some people were just looking for a handout. Others sincerely wanted help. Some were filled with rage, some on the verge of violence, others on the verge of collapse. No matter their condition, I tried my best to treat them with respect. I tried to be helpful and welcoming. If I did my job right, I could point them in a positive direction. I found that the feeling of usefulness was, in and of itself, rewarding.

All this was good. All this was forward motion. But all this did not prepare me for a statement made by one of the directors of ARC.

"Kim," he said, "it's time for you to move on."

By *move on* he meant "move out."

You'd think that would have made me happy, but no; I was terrified. It might have been the same kind of fear a prisoner has after being released from serving a lengthy sentence. The Salvation Army, the ARC, the meetings, the dorm, my room, my jobs as a driver and intake counselor, the fellowship—they provided comfort. They provided a safe place. The outside world still did not seem all that safe. For well over a year, I had lived in a womb of recovery. I had been protected, nurtured, fed by wisdom. I had learned to speak my pain. And most important, I was no longer high.

The thought of leaving brought on an assault of anxiety.

Could I make it out there?

Could I face the harsh reality of living in a place whose prime focus would not be rehabilitation?

And more to the point, did I really believe that I was rehabilitated?

"That's not the right question," said one of the ARC's elders. "Who knows when any of us are truly rehabilitated? What does that even mean? Rehabilitation is an ongoing process. It never stops. Complete rehabilitation means complete reunification with our higher power. But, aside from a few holy men and women, none of us get there. So, it's back to the only mantra that keeps us steady: *One day at a time.* If you can make it outside of the ARC for twenty-four hours, then you can make it another twenty-four hours. Don't jump ahead. The future is all about fear, the past all about regret, but right now you're looking good to me, Kim. And this 'right now' doesn't need to go away. Make 'right now' a permanent condition, a permanent state of mind. 'Right now' is all we really have. So get your ass out of here and find a place to live, right now."

28

LETTING GO

I set a date for leaving the Sally.

And then stayed beyond that date.

Then I set another date, only to bust through that one as well.

Letting go was tougher than I'd thought.

Motivation came in the form of another twelve-step elder who said, "You're not leaving the program. You're taking the program with you. The program isn't just a building or a meeting. The program lives inside you, like God. And just like God is everything and everywhere, so is the program."

I began to understand the difference between the physical and the metaphysical. The physical building that served as a refuge from the storm of my addiction was something I could touch. But the spirit that informed my heart was metaphysical. It couldn't be touched, but man, it could be felt. It could be expanded. And away from that building, there were meetings all over Detroit where I could renew that spirit.

———————

There was another building that contained a spirit that enhanced my life. The building marked a beautiful crossroads where my mother's recovery and my own recovery intersected. Initial credit must be given to my dad.

He had brought home audiotapes that a colleague had given him. Mom devoured them. One was a series of lectures, *It's All Within Your Reach* by Michael Wickett, a motivational speaker with strong positive energy. Wickett was connected to the Church of Today, later called Renaissance Unity Interfaith Fellowship, where Jack Boland was founder and minister. The congregation invited lecturers like Wayne Dyer, Og Mandino, and Les Brown. Mom began going to the services, where it was all about spiritual renewal. I had been watching her growth from afar and knew the church had played a significant role in her transformation. I accepted her invitation to join her for one of the Sunday services.

Twenty-three miles north of downtown Detroit in Warren, the complex was impressive. The megachurch covered seventy-seven thousand square feet and seated some three thousand worshippers. There was a bookstore that stocked an extensive variety of New Thought tomes. There were literally dozens of twelve-step meetings for people challenged by addictions ranging from alcohol to drugs to sex to codependency.

I saw Unity, as did my mother, as an extension of the culture of recovery. Her own recovery inspired mine. Since she'd gotten sober, she had completely turned her life around. Her entrepreneurial energy, long dormant, was ignited. Mom had already begun a business selling gift baskets store-to-store and door-to-door. At Unity, she met a woman who worked with Mary Kay cosmetics and urged her to do the same. Eventually Mom became a high-ranking Mary Kay manager, traveling to conventions and leading seminars. She kept her basket business as well, selling her own products along with Mary Kay's.

This was a time when I rebonded with Mom, when she was able to speak about her traumatic past, which, in turn, helped clarify parts of my own history.

I resonated with Unity for several reasons. The congregation included all age groups and ethnicities. There was no choir but superb solo singers. The spiritual lessons were neither doctrinaire nor narrow-minded. There was never an air of exclusivity. There was no proselytizing. The preaching was never heavy-handed. You didn't hear one specific theology being upheld and others diminished. The preaching augmented what I continued to learn in my twelve-step meetings: that personal growth comes with the ever-expanding consciousness of love, honesty, and service. The more we learn to truly give and receive love, the more we grow.

All this added to my overall search for ways in which I could become more myself. If, as I was taught, we all contain divinity, how can I access that divinity? How can I manifest it?

As I sat in church, especially during moments of silent meditation, I increasingly knew that my search was leading me back to the one thing that had always carried a sense of mystical beauty to me: music.

29

GRINDING IT OUT

I had many jobs. I caught the bus to work the night shift at an auto supply firm and then, during the day, rode a bike to my gig at Mc-Crory's Five and Dime. As Mom's had for her, my work ethic had kicked in. But my professional status was still nonexistent. I wanted that to change. I wanted to be a professional musician.

I thought John Penn could help. Years after our Wild Pair days, I met John through Brian O'Neal. John was a different kind of brother. He didn't fit easily into any category. He had a Steve Jobs vibe. He was a nerd, but with an edge. He was enrolled at Wayne State, on track to be a doctor. Yet his true ambition was musical, not medical. He wanted to conquer the music world. He had trouble shaking off his parents' ambitions for him. Knowing they had a brilliant son, they saw him in medical or law school. He had an aptitude for both, but he saw his future in producing hit songs. He heard the things I'd been doing with Brian and thought we had potential. Brian was situated in his own place. I wasn't. John was kind enough to let me move into his house after I left the Sally.

As an instrumentalist, Brian was a virtuoso. John was not. But John could get by. On keyboards, he could construct chords and melodies. He understood theory and read and wrote with impressive skill. He was also a strong-headed alpha, and, although I was far behind him in life's journey, we would often butt heads. I had ideas of my own.

Yet I was careful to maintain our relationship. It excited me to be with someone with overt ambition. I realized the benefit of absorbing the aspirational energy of others. I knew John was going places, and I wanted to be part of his trip.

Along with Brian, we often worked together. For long periods of time, though, especially late at night, I also worked alone at the keyboard. As a writer and singer, I was slowly trying to find a voice and style of my own. That voice and style were then, and always would be, based on experimentation. I was bending a note this way and that way. Singing high and singing low. Singing forcefully, singing tenderly. I wasn't interested in copying anything that was already out there. I knew I was different. As much as I loved the music of my childhood, I knew that the sensibilities of, say, Michael and Prince did not match mine. So my search continued.

Once I sat down at the blessed keyboard, I might not get up for two, three, or four hours. I was looking for the lost chord. The very act of constructing chords, seeking harmonies, creating clusters of sounds, was as prayerful as it was musical. I was persistent and patient, which was strange, because that wasn't usually the case any other time. But the keyboard anchored me. I couldn't stay away from it. In the interplay between silence and sound, the keyboard held the mystery I needed to uncover.

———————

Singing was just as important.

While I was living at John's, he had begun working with UNV—Universal Nubian Voices—a four-man vocal group with excellent lead singers and extremely tight harmonies. This was when Motown had just released Boys II Men's *Cooleyhighharmony* and Bell Biv DeVoe was flying high. Old-school R & B combined with New Jack Swing grooves and hip-hop samples were all the rage.

I studied the process. John was into everything I was into: meticulously sculpting sound. At one point he became interested in my voice, as unformed as it was. He, Brian, and I continued working together. John produced a four-song recording of me and released it as an extended-play album called *Can't Figure U Out*. The nasal tone I had adopted on that recording, to my ears, didn't feel quite right. But I could hardly get mad at a local jazz station, the beloved WJZZ, when they played it a couple of times. Who doesn't get a kick out of hearing themselves on the radio?

During this time, I opened twice for Meshell Ndegeocello, a great pioneer of neo-soul. *Plantation Lullabies*, her debut album, was groundbreaking, the level of her musicianship remarkably high. I loved and respected her work.

So, it was especially humbling that my initial performance consisted of a microphone in front of a boom box playing a cassette of my instrumental track. The second time I opened for Meshell we played the Royal Oak Music Theatre and I had at least upgraded to a live makeshift band.

Interesting that my first play was on a jazz station. *Can't Figure U Out* was hardly jazz. This was my initial introduction to the conundrum that hundreds of singers have faced. Where does R & B end and jazz begin? Every great R & B singer, from Sam Cooke to

Aretha Franklin to Stevie Wonder, employs jazz phrasing, just as every great jazz singer, from Louis Armstrong to Billie Holiday to Bobby McFerrin, is rooted in the blues. Not to mention singers who have enjoyed pop success like Nat Cole and Nancy Wilson, who, without their foundation in jazz and blues, would never have carved out an identity of their own.

An identity of my own—that's what I wanted. The negative voices in my head weren't as persistent but they were still around. *You'll never find your own style. You'll never get over in the music business. You'll never be good enough.* And though those voices shook me up, they were mitigated by indisputable facts: I was making records. Some people were coming to my shows. I was getting somewhere. I was getting closer to finding an authentic sound.

If there was a parallel to my sitting at the piano for hours at a time, looking for the lost chord, it was my singing into a tape recorder hoping to find a fragment of what would become my musical voice.

How do you find that chord? How do you find that voice?

The process is mysterious. At the start of the journey, I was both eager and confused. The genre dilemma—*Am I jazz? Am I R & B?*—was minor. If I was categorized, even wrongly categorized, who cared? At least I was being heard. But if I didn't like what I was hearing, if I wasn't happy with my identity as an artist, what could I do about it?

The easiest solution to self-identity came when John put the name Kem on the record. He had always heard "Kim" as "Kem" and presumed that was my name. I liked the variation. I found it distinctive and kept it. But then came the old question "What's in a name?" Not much if you don't have a strong sense of self.

The twelve-step meetings helped. The meetings always help. They continue to help because their format counteracts self-obsession. In a sixty-minute meeting, I'd listen for fifty-five minutes and speak for five. I'd realize that this search for self was universal. Feeling lost was the norm. Feeling unsettled was fine. Being uncomfortable with your progress, whether personal or professional, was part of the human condition. Of the many mantras offered, *Progress, not perfection* maybe mattered most.

I needed that mantra because the longer I lived outside the walls of a recovery shelter, the more I saw myself falling into the trap of impatience. The key was to accept whatever progress I was making, as insignificant as it might have seemed.

Because I felt the need for a place of my own, I moved out of John's to a little apartment around the corner on 6 Mile Road. I was feeling especially vulnerable, maybe because a car hit my bike—I was lucky only to be bruised—or maybe because I got mugged at the bus stop. When the muggers saw I had barely enough for bus fare, they were pissed. Again, I was lucky they didn't blow my brains out. I felt like I was attracting negative energy. But what could I do about it?

Go to a meeting. Admit my vulnerability. Admit my fear. Stay sober and keep trying to do the next right thing, one day at a time.

30

TEMPTED

A man invites a woman to a Kenny Rogers Christmas concert at the Fox Theatre in Detroit. The man—me—has liked Kenny Rogers since he and his mom listened to "The Gambler" when he was a kid. He came across a quote from Kenny that stayed with him: "You either do what everyone else is doing and you do it better, or you do what no one else is doing and you don't invite comparison." As a young man whose career ambitions had started to blossom, those words meant a lot.

The young woman, who is white, is a natural beauty. There's a mystery behind her eyes. Like the man, she is newly invested in spirituality. Her own spirit is vivacious. She's a brunette, a talker and a charmer who's held in high regard by her friends. She has a job, goes to college, and loves music. Her name is Michelle Clark.

The December night is chilly but the festive feeling is warm. The Fox Theatre is all decked out with holly and wreaths. A huge

Christmas tree illuminates the lobby. The eager crowd is dressed in overcoats, scarves, and mittens. In her tight red wool cap decorated with Santa's elves, Michelle is adorable. She wears no makeup. That only adds to her appeal. My one blue suit may not be new, but my stingy-brim hat, cocked to the side, gives me a little swag. At least Michelle seems to think so.

We take our seats as Kenny takes over. He comes out in a white suit that matches his close-cropped white beard. He's relaxed and amiable, and with the backing of a big band, he sings his huge hits, like "Lady" and "Islands in the Stream." After intermission, the show takes a decidedly Christmas turn. Now in a red suit with a vest, he sings, in addition to carols, seasonal standards like "White Christmas" and "Winter Wonderland." We leave feeling great.

That same night, over coffee and cake, we discuss a book we've just read, *The Sermon on the Mount: The Key to Success in Life* by Emmet Fox, a man considered to be one of the world's greatest metaphysical teachers. The book is all about being connected to God as a way to better our daily journey. Michelle is as excited about the book as I am. On our to-do list, self-improvement is item number one.

———

Over the months, our relationship deepened. It was Michelle's idea to see the Alvin Ailey American Dance Theater as well as the Dance Theatre of Harlem. I appreciated the beauty of the bodies in motion, their relationship to the music and story. In one ballet, *Medea*, I was stunned—and shocked—by the final scene, in which the ballerina, in a costume constructed to look like octopus tenacles, goes on a murderous rampage, killing, among others, her own children. It was my first experience with the power of ancient Greek mythology.

On Valentine's Day, I wanted to take Michelle to Benihana, the

Japanese steak house. Before going there, I had studied the menu because I had no more than $30 to spend. I knew if I ordered the cheapest thing on the menu and nothing to drink, I could slide by. Barely. But because I didn't want to give the appearance of being the broke-ass man that I was, I maintained my cool. "Order anything you want, baby," I said, all the time sweating that if she ordered a fancy dessert, I'd have to borrow money from her to pay for it. Fortunately, she bypassed dessert and I walked out of there with change to spare.

───────

Mom wasn't thrilled with my relationship with Michelle, but I understood her attitude about Black men dating white women. I was attracted to women of various hues and backgrounds. It would be silly for me to stand in judgment of interracial relationships. I know they can be healthy and long-lasting. However, I'm also aware that, here in America, the Black man/white woman dynamic has deep implications for both parties. It's never simple because, given our history, sociopolitical concerns are inevitably part of the mix.

Did Michelle's whiteness make her more attractive to me? Did her romantic interest in me help me feel more accepted by a culture with a murderous history of prejudice and subjugation? On Michelle's end, did my Blackness make me more attractive to her? By embracing me, was she working off white guilt?

All those questions are legitimate, and they certainly all came into play. Yet the heart of the matter was romantic. I dug her. She dug me. She was in college, curious, energetic. She loved people and people loved her. Her parents had been divorced for a while and she lived with her mom, who worked for a nonprofit. Michelle was cool.

At Thanksgiving, Mom relented and allowed me to invite Michelle to dinner. It so happened that Dad's mom was visiting from West Palm Beach. Grandma Maurice was a far more pleasant person in Michigan than in Florida. She brought levity to our home. With lighthearted humor, she'd argue vehemently for the superiority of pumpkin pie over sweet potato pie. Grandma was a piece of work. She could be fun. At the same time, I had to warn Michelle to be on guard; Grandma might well take issue with my dating a white woman.

Yet during dinner there was, in fact, no difficulty. The conversation was lively, with everyone on their best behavior. At one point, Michelle was so happy to have the proverbial ice broken when it came to meeting my family that she said, "Kem, your grandmother is so wonderful. I don't know what you were so worried about."

Naturally, Grandma wanted to know why I had been worried. What had I told Michelle about her? Why was I saying bad things about her? Seeing her mistake, Michelle jumped back in to say that I had only good things to say about Grandma, but by then the cat was out of the bag. I was jumping through hoops to assuage my grandmother before things got out of hand. Michelle meant no harm. She had a good heart and, if anything, was just exuberant about being welcomed into the bosom of my family.

I was stoked that a song I had worked on, "Tempted," made it onto *Something's Goin' On*, the UNV album John was producing. Though it didn't make me any money, the fact that it got placed reinforced my confidence in my songwriting ability.

Workwise, forget it. I got fired from my job at the auto supply place, and my gig at McCrory's Five and Dime only paid $3.35 an hour. As a result, I didn't have enough money to pay my rent and was staring at an eviction notice. I ended up renting a room in a house with a couple of guys in recovery. That was fine, but I would have much rather been living with Michelle.

She and I put together our resources—I'd found a job at Rite Aid—and we got a little apartment in Inkster, a blue-collar, factory-heavy small city just outside Detroit. And while I loved Michelle's company, I wasn't ready to commit. My life wasn't as solid as I would have liked and I wasn't happy having to scrimp and save to pay rent. I wanted music to be a means to financial gain. More than that, I felt like it was my calling, but it didn't seem like it was ever going to happen. What did end up happening was something that would change my world forever:

Michelle and I got pregnant.

31

MIXED EMOTIONS

Michelle wanted to have the baby, and so did I. Her mother was supportive. My mother was concerned. She still had misgivings about my being with a white woman. The idea of becoming a father was equally exciting and frightening. It meant I had to man up. I left Rite Aid, and borrowing Michelle's car, I drove to my new nine-to-five at American Blind and Wallpaper Factory. They put me in customer service. That meant making sure the customers were happy—solving problems involving installation and billing. I was Mr. Problem Solver. Every night I went home with a headache.

The headache went away on March 8, 1995, the day our precious daughter, Troi, was born. I was blessed to be there to cut the umbilical cord. Blessed to see this baby's beauty, this infant with a head full of curly hair. I loved holding her in my arms. Loved seeing Michelle bond with the baby. Loved bonding with the baby myself. Loved keeping Troi in my life, then, now, and forever.

Michelle and I went our separate ways six months after Troi was born. The breakup wasn't easy, but fortunately we stayed friends. It was all on me. I lacked the emotional intelligence to truly engage with the heart and mind of another person. I had not learned the art of compromise. I could not negotiate the volatility of my moods due to my frustration that, at age twenty-eight, I was not the man I wanted to be. Not even close.

But I stayed close by. I visited often, making sure that Troi understood that she had a father. My mother came around as well. At the first sight of her granddaughter, her old attitudes seemed to melt away. She became loving and attentive.

———

Eventually, I was tempted to get out of Dodge and move to Atlanta, the new R & B hot spot where John Penn and Brian O'Neal had recently relocated. It was in Atlanta where LaFace Records, formed by writer/producers LA Reid and Kenny "Babyface" Edmonds, was turning out hits for everyone from TLC to Toni Braxton to Outkast to Usher.

Meanwhile, John was making headway. Before leaving Detroit for Atlanta, he had secured a record deal for UNV with Maverick Records, Madonna's label. I dreamed that maybe I, too, could get signed to a major label.

I went down for a few days and saw that what they were saying was true. The studios were popping. The mansions in Buckhead were enticing. Positive energy, productivity in abundance. Atlanta looked like the promised land, America's most prosperous Chocolate City. Atlanta represented musical success. How could I not be a part of that?

Beyond his musical involvement with John, Brian was working

as a computer programmer with Coca-Cola. He was driving around town in a white Mustang convertible. John was busy in the studio. Neither of them urged me to join them, but neither did they discourage me. If I made the move, I felt certain we could renew our relationship and work up fresh material.

I wasn't the kind of man who would run out on his infant child, but I was the kind of man who could rationalize. I could make a plan. A month in Atlanta, and then a month in Detroit. I'd split my time between a personal home and a professional life. I could manage it. No problem.

Except for the quiet, knowing voice inside me that said, "You're bullshitting yourself. If you move to Atlanta, you won't come back. You'll throw yourself into that world and never leave. You'll keep postponing those trips back to Detroit. You'll forget your baby. You'll see your child once every six months, if that often."

I saw myself doing what millions of men had done before me: putting my own wants and needs first.

I came close to doing just that, but something said no. Inkster may not have been Atlanta, but Inkster was where I needed to be. Dealing with customer complaints at American Blind and Wallpaper was where I needed to be.

32

THE MASKS OF A MAN

I began a song that said . . .

The masks of a man
The marks, bruises
Pain and scars
The smiles hiding
Just who you are
The masks of a man
Covering up
Playing it cool
Burying the fear of
Playing the fool

I was still wearing a mask that men, uncertain or confused, tend to wear. On the outside, I was maintaining my cool. On the inside, I was straining. I desperately wanted to get someplace with my music even as I knew that I had to make a living to help support my child.

Leaving Troi wasn't an option, so I was still living in Inkster. I liked being a hands-on dad, changing diapers, giving baths, and later taking her to preschool. Now that I had a daughter to take care of, I realized that working as a customer service rep at the blind and wallpaper firm wasn't going to be enough. I needed a second gig. Humility was required. Humility is always required. Humility meant taking whatever gig I could get.

Knowing I was in dire financial straits and looking to help, Mom suggested that Mary Kay might be a lucrative path for me as well. I had reservations. It didn't seem like the most manly way to make a living, but my mindset at the time could be summed up in three succinct words: what the hell. Mom made it possible for me to secure a $2,000 loan that would let me buy an ample supply of Mary Kay products to sell. I was reluctant but ready. Or at least I thought I was.

The day that $2,000 check arrived, something began shifting. I looked at that piece of paper. I counted the zeros. I was in my car ready to roll. But somehow I didn't roll in the right direction. Instead of heading east to place a Mary Kay order with Mom, I found myself moving west on Cherry Hill Road toward Canton. Why? Because the Arnoldt Williams music store was in Canton.

The little birdie sitting on my right shoulder said, "Turn around and do as you promised. Go get those Mary Kay products and start making some decent money. Be practical."

The little birdie on my left shoulder said, "Be creative. Be who you were born to be. Take this money and buy a keyboard."

I stayed on course to Canton.

Once I reached Arnoldt Williams, I made a beeline for the Ensoniq MR76. Of course, the ultimate dream was a Steinway piano, since that was the instrument I'd first played in the music room back in high school. That dream, though, was wildly unrealistic. The Ensoniq MR76 was within reach. It was the electric keyboard I'd been fingering for months, a keyboard in line with the ones Brian had introduced me to. The MR76 was a sequencer, meaning I could program drums and add instruments on top, but, in truth, I was never very good at it. Yet I could play with chords—and did so for hours—and I could adjust and readjust the tone until I was satisfied.

My inability to realize the potential of the instrument turned out to be key. If I had done so, I would never have needed a band. That need would ultimately and profoundly shape my sound. In the end, I'm grateful for my technical inadequacy. The presence of a live band would become a major blessing.

Years passed before that band was formed. Meanwhile, driving home with the Ensoniq in the trunk, the little birdie who'd told me to pick up the Mary Kay products had disappeared. The other birdie who had sent me to Canton was chirping like mad. All my doubts had disappeared. I had what I wanted. The purchase of the keyboard felt like the key to a new life. Growth. An unexplored world ahead. I couldn't keep my hands off the thing. I clung to it. The Ensoniq encompassed every metaphor imaginable: a church for praying, a schoolroom for learning, a temple for meditation.

And all the time—countless days and countless hours—my search for the lost chord continued.

Certain chords did resonate with an emotional impact that felt like love. Those chords expressed a beauty coursing through me. But to turn those chords into song—and to give them a voice that rang true—would take years of exploration.

The exploration felt urgent and necessary. Even more urgent and necessary, though, was paying bills. I held on to my customer service job telling people how to measure for inside- and outside-mounted blinds, but I needed more income—and fast.

Mom wasn't thrilled that I'd passed up Mary Kay but never chastised me. She was pleased that I remained industrious. I kept looking for work.

"You've got the kind of personality that would make a good waiter," said a friend.

"What does that mean?" I asked.

"You can turn on the charm."

I never saw myself as a charmer, but the idea of serving food didn't bother me. Plus, I could work the customer service gig during the day and wait tables at night. I got hired at a seafood restaurant and fell into the routine relatively quickly. I was fast on my feet and happy to be serving up the fried shrimp and flounder.

One night saxophonist David McMurray walked in with his wife, Garzelle, to celebrate his birthday. I hadn't seen Dave since my down-and-out days. I was glad to see him. After what had happened at Sound Suite Studios, I was especially glad that he could see me sober. The evening was beautiful.

No matter how late I worked, I never went to sleep before sitting at the keyboard. My songs were out there somewhere in the ether. I tried playing them home, praying them home, calling to them as best I could. One sounded like what would eventually become "Love Calls." Several other bits and pieces of songs lived in my head and in my keyboard. They remained nameless—for the moment.

When my beat-up car bit the dust, Michelle's mom had a friend who sold me a used, un-air-conditioned Toyota Tercel with a manual transmission. A friend taught me how to drive a stick on a Sunday afternoon. Monday I drove it to work.

Another friend—a cook at the seafood joint—pointed me in another positive direction.

"On my off days I work at the Ritz-Carlton in Dearborn," he said. "I can put in a good word for you. I think you'll fit right in. You've got that upscale, fine-dining vibe."

I was down with that. The application process was thorough and acceptance was considered an achievement. When it came to waitering, the Ritz-Carlton was a major upgrade, an introduction to five-star service. I was hired to work in the banquets department. The linen tablecloths, the imported silverware, the fresh flowers . . . all had to be placed just so. The impact on me was enormous. I learned to properly fold a napkin and uncork a bottle of fine wine. I experienced the satisfaction of wearing shirts with French cuffs. I wore black bow ties—not clip-ons, the kind I had to tie. I embraced this new sense of style. When someone said, "Thank you," instead of saying, "You're welcome," I replied, "My pleasure." I dug the refinement. I dug the sophistication. The Ritz was the embodiment of the prestigious lifestyle to which I aspired.

At the Ritz-Carlton, I was thrust into another world. That culture of excellence has stuck with me even to this day, where I've learned striving to deliver excellence applies to more than serving customers at a hotel. It applies to serving my music. It applies to serving everyone.

Some might say I was putting on another mask—a mask of respectability. But I didn't see it that way. It felt completely natural. It put me at ease.

Today you may be working there, but someday you'll be staying there!

33

THE GOSPEL TRUTH

My spiritual life was sustained by ongoing recovery meetings as well as the church Mom had introduced me to. Although it was an hour away from Inkster, many Sundays I'd go get Troi, buckle her up in the backseat, and, once I was seated in the sanctuary, hold her in my lap while I took in the messages of hope.

I had spiritual aspirations. I also had career aspirations. But I never connected the two. Back then, I didn't understand that spirit is connected to everything. I was amazed to see how that worked out on a practical level.

I didn't take the job at the Ritz-Carlton for either spiritual or professional reasons. It was just a good job. Yet that job put me in a place where a few brief exchanges changed the course of my life.

I was working a banquet at the hotel when I saw Marianne Williamson, who had become the new senior minister at the Church of Today. It had been many years since I started attending the church with Mom and Dad, but my allegiance remained strong. I attended regularly, and Ms. Williamson's sermons were among the most moving I had heard. Her book *A Return to Love*, celebrated by Oprah Winfrey, had become an international sensation, along with her work with *A Course in Miracles*.

On this particular evening she was seated at a table with Ortheia Barnes, the legendary Detroit R & B/jazz singer who often sang at the church. I was serving them coffee when I found the courage to say, "My parents and I have been attending your church for years." I told Ortheia how much I enjoyed her rendition of Elton John's "Circle of Life." I also mentioned that I was an aspiring artist.

"That's wonderful," said Ms. Williamson. "We're putting together a choir. Why don't you call the church tomorrow? Ask for Lori Onachuk, our musical director. She'll be auditioning singers next week. She'll be happy to meet you."

———

The audition was more arduous than I had anticipated. Lori explained that sixteen singers would be chosen. That sounds like a lot, but looking around I saw at least twice that many, all of whom came from the city's best Top 40 bands. Competition was stiff, and I was proud to be selected. I was both humbled and honored to be in a choir, called the Gospel Truth, where standards were sky-high.

I didn't see it as a setting where I'd experience a seismic shift in my life, yet it turned out to be just that. I was given a solo spot— "Thank You, Lord"—that was well received. During a Thanksgiving service, I was set to sing the song during the offering. That's when our choir director Ed Gooch casually suggested that I first say a few words about my life. That was outside my usual character. Sharing at twelve-step meetings was one thing. It's private. This was public. Not to mention a church. What did I have to say and how was I going to say it?

Despite my trepidation, I let myself go. I was transparent. I talked about my gratitude for being sober. About being kicked out of my house. About being homeless. About being locked up. About feeling worthless. Hopeless. About my long journey of recovery. I can't recall the exact words I spoke. I was in the moment and I expressed my whole heart.

The congregation lost it. The reaction was incredible. It was a pivotal moment. It became the transformative template for how I'd connect with my audiences for years to come. I realized that through music, I could serve. I could do ministry. I could be an ambassador of love. An ambassador of God.

Suddenly, I saw my art take a different turn. Before, music had been one thing and recovery had been another. Now they were joined.

On other Sundays, Marianne would invite guests like Father Leo and Michael Beckwith to speak on what some would call New Age pathways to God. While fundamental Christianity, which I embrace completely, would frown on these teachings, I didn't. I had witnessed God's love, his grace, and his mercy firsthand. I heard them advocating love. Their advocation was free of judgment. Their messages of self-acceptance and an all-embracing God of grace were just what I needed to hear.

I began recognizing the divinity of music. I saw that romantic music—secular music—could contain the same yearning for wholeness as sacred music. Romantic music was sacred, just as sacred music could be called romantic. God draws us to his heart. I began hearing God's inspiration in all music. I began understanding God as music and music as God.

———

The choir was an unexpected gateway. For example, the choir director had a friend who ran a wedding band in need of a lead male vocalist. I auditioned and got the gig. The experience proved invaluable. The band was superb. There was a crisp horn section and a tight rhythm section. Naturally, it was all covers. The singing was demanding. At weddings in fancy country clubs or parties in modest recreation halls, it was two women and myself switching leads and harmonizing background vocals to a wide variety of songs. We played everything from "My Girl" and "Under the Boardwalk" to "This Is How We Do It" and our infamous version of Santana's "Smooth." And of course, no wedding reception would be complete without Sister Sledge's faithful "We Are Family."

It was on-the-job training. The aim was simple: keep the vibe pumping, keep the folks dancing, keep the party moving. It was the first time I had no choice but to embrace a musical mandate that came down to a single word: *Entertain!*

34

LIKE BLOOD THROUGH MY VEINS

I search my heart
And start to pray
For music to sustain me
One more day
For harmonies that heal
Loneliness and pain
And melodies that move
Like blood through my veins

I was writing whatever came to mind. Some words turned into actual compositions. Some didn't. Because no matter how grateful I was to be singing in a wedding band, I felt I had something original to say that could only be said in songs of my own. The long, arduous process of writing my first complete album had begun.

When I started this five-year journey, I didn't have an official title for the album. Though I did remember having a conversation with a recovery friend of mine a few years earlier. I'd told him I was going to name my debut album *Kemistry*. In the meantime, the alchemy had started, but the music wasn't even close to jelling. That process would consume me for the second half of the 1990s. To unearth the music buried in my heart was as excruciating as it was exhilarating.

I had never formally studied my musical roots. Those roots, though, had formed me. Country blues and city blues, the slick jump bands of the 1940s, the raucous R & B of the 1950s, the rock-steady soul of the 1960s, the far-out fusion of the 1970s, the Michael Jackson and Prince phenomena of the 1980s. I ingested it all. Tania Maria's *Love Explosion*, Bob James and David Sanborn's *Double Vision*. The influences were rich and varied. Maybe that's why it took me so long to formulate what I wanted to say and how to say it, play it, and sing it. My tools were basic: the keyboard, a four-track from the Music Castle on Woodward Avenue, and a microphone. It's no accident that the first demo I developed that actually appeared on *Kemistry* was "Love Calls."

I say that because at the same time music was swelling my heart, so was the love I felt for a woman. We met at "This Place," a song on *Kemistry* whose subtitle was "Church of Today," the original name of Renaissance Unity.

The lyrics say . . .

There's a fountain of hope
Living water for each of us
There are rivers of dreams
Flowing through the heartache of this place
There are children that flower the trees
There are voices of people who need
This place
There's sorrow and sadness here
But there's heaven and sunshine too . . .

Clearly, I had written a love song to a church, and, because my heart was so open, it makes sense that in this same church I would find myself falling for a woman. Her name was Sarah. She was a member of the Renaissance Unity congregation.

I saw her sitting there every Sunday and hoped she saw me. When I sang, I hoped she heard me. Hoped she liked me. Hoped that she might be half as fascinated by me as I was by her. She had long brunette hair and bluish green-gray eyes. Her olive complexion reminded me of Rebecca from my childhood, the Jewish girl I met at fifteen. Sarah was also Jewish. She fit into the Rebecca mold. She looked like the lady I had been searching for. I can't say why. Did I sense her spiritual curiosity? Her openness? Or was it just a question of her physical attractiveness?

All I know is that I very much wanted to catch Sarah's attention. I caught it on a Sunday when sunflowers were being sold as part of a fundraiser. I bought a bunch and, just as she was leaving church, offered them to her. Sarah smiled and accepted them graciously. After exchanging a few words, we realized we knew some of the same people.

We chatted amicably. She introduced me to her niece Chelsea, whom she brought to church regularly. Sarah was studying law at Wayne State University. She asked about my work. She was a little surprised that I was a waiter at the Ritz-Carlton. She figured I had found full-time work as a musician.

"Not yet," I said.

I did mention, though, that I had a gig with my quintet at a place called the Bonfire Grill in Livonia, twenty minutes from downtown Detroit. In between my work as a wedding band singer and waiting tables at the Ritz-Carlton, a random gig was a place to try out my original material. The gig wasn't as polished as the performances Sarah was accustomed to on Sunday mornings. As a performer and songwriter, I was still a work in progress. Nevertheless, I invited her to come check me out.

I convinced the owner of the restaurant to hire us to play three forty-five-minute sets with twenty-minute breaks. The pay was $50 a man. The fact that I was able to secure this gig still amazes me. We only played a rotation of five of my original songs from what would eventually become the *Kemistry* album: "Love Calls," "Say," "This Place," "Miss You," and "Inside."

The night would break down like this: For the first half of each set, we would play all five of our songs, but only as instrumentals with each band member taking a super-extended solo. For the second half of the set, we would play the same five songs, only this time I would actually sing, after which we would take a break and repeat. Detroit hustle was on full display.

Naturally I was glad to see Sarah. Her hair was pulled back into a ponytail. She dressed stylishly but simply. She was low-key and down-to-earth. After the last set, she stayed around. She was friendly without being chatty, curious without being nosy.

Sarah complimented me on my performance. She said I was a good bandleader. That surprised me, because I didn't see myself that way. I considered my musicians colleagues helping me find the groove. I rented and hauled the equipment and scheduled rehearsals. I told Sarah that I was essentially conducting a public workshop to flesh out my original material. She said that, to her, the songs felt finished. I said I was still worried about whether this new material was worthwhile. According to her, I had nothing to worry about.

Our relationship blossomed.

Talking to Sarah on the phone quickly became my favorite pastime. She'd tell me about her law classes. Some of her profs were great, others not so much. I'd give her the rundown on the customers I served at the Ritz-Carlton. Some were generous; others never tipped. We made each other laugh. Sunday sermons at Unity were also always on the table for discussion. Sarah had insights that made me think. She wasn't just smart, she was genuine. She was gentle but assertive, cautious but confident. We talked for hours.

Our friendship was solid before we became lovers. We were on the same page. Sarah's motivation to succeed academically added to my motivation to succeed musically. Everything was good. Or so I thought.

I think there are many factors baked into the cake of dating outside of one's race. In my case, I was unconsciously looking for women who reminded me of Rebecca, the Jewish girl from my childhood who for years was the center of both my affection and my infatuation. There was also this idea that being with a white woman would somehow tilt the scales of acceptance in my favor. That somehow it made me better and softened the shame-filled feelings of not being good enough. Being too dark. Being too broke.

I do not believe that we need to defend our reasons for choosing the people we love. I do believe, though, we need to try to understand them. Relationships that lack this understanding are doomed to fail. I wish I'd had a greater understanding of the complexity of my feelings at the start of my relationship with Sarah.

During the gestation years for *Kemistry*, Sarah was an integral part of my life. Like me, she was a searcher. She understood that these songs that I had been working on for so long went beneath the surface. I was excavating my soul. She encouraged that excavation and, in many ways, contributed to it.

But was Sarah my soul mate? At the time, it seemed so. It seemed like we were moving in the same direction. I didn't see the obstacles ahead. I didn't see the challenges. There was so much I didn't see — or didn't want to see — because my mind was focused, more than anything, on the music.

35

MATTER OF TIME

How do you balance persistence with patience? How do you temper eagerness with care? I cared more about *Kemistry* than anything I'd ever done. The obsession was full-blown. I even found a way to work on the material at, of all places, the Ritz-Carlton.

Before big dinners, there was always a reception where a pianist played quiet standards on one of three Steinway grands throughout the hotel. While still serving as a waiter, I was hired to play several such receptions. The pay was $75. They didn't seem to mind that I wasn't doing a rendition of "Stella by Starlight" but instead was focused on "Inside" or "Love Calls" or "You Are," all original songs that would make their way onto the *Kemistry* album. In order to not draw attention away from the cocktail cordiality, I played and sang softly. But as I did so, I was always editing lyrics and modifying melodies. Sometimes a guest would stop at the piano and smile. But mostly I was ignored. That was fine with me. I liked being trapped inside my own head with my music. Ironically, I was there to entertain. But I was continuing my search for the lost chord.

The *Kemistry* album would become a statement of who I was and who I wanted to be. Bringing it to life was often a lonely process. My musical style wasn't similar to that of any other music being made at the time. That isn't to say I wasn't aware of what was going on in R & B or what was being called smooth jazz. I respected everyone from Destiny's Child to Kirk Whalum. At the same time, I was in my own lane. In fact, my work was so deeply personal I wondered whether listeners would relate. I had a very singular story to tell. I also had a very particular voice. The more I sang, the more I recognized my voice as an instrument. Wordless sounds were part of my style.

My ability to commit these sounds and stories to tape came through an unexpected source. I had fooled with credit cards for years, borrowing from Peter to pay Paul, but I didn't receive an American Express Gold Card through manipulation. I got it because I paid off the $2,000 keyboard loan. I believe there was an anointing on that credit card that spoke to me and said, "Take these tunes you've written and record them."

And so I did.

The first song—the one that would ultimately kick off *Kemistry*— was "Matter of Time," a meditation on the miracle of recovery. The jam also served to remind me that, for all my endless revisions, it was time to finally commit these compositions to tape. But my funds only went so far. I could buy much-needed equipment, rent out rehearsal space, and pay my band, but the cost of a first-rate studio was out of reach. My homegrown demos would not get me a deal. The only alternative was to record live.

I couldn't have done the live recording without Toya Hankins, my manager. She pulled it together at Café Aroma, an east-side coffeehouse where the mood was intimate. Toya drew a crowd, not based on my popularity—I had none—but by scheduling the show on her birthday. A natural-born networker, Toya was much loved in the community. Turning our recording into part of her birthday celebration guaranteed us a full house.

The crowd was enthusiastic. I was not. The result of my efforts didn't seem to measure up to what was living in my head. The session wasn't bad, the songs were all there, but I suspected I could get a better result by recording in a controlled environment. I needed to find a professional studio.

At the very least, I had put myself out there. That had to count for something. And, though I wasn't completely thrilled with my vocal performance, I could see the promise of what could be.

I was thirty-three; the year was 2000.

"Matter of Time" applied to my relationship with Sarah. Understandably, she wanted to be married. She wanted a deeper commitment. I was dragging my feet.

Mom and Dad had met Sarah many times. They knew how serious we were. Sarah and I were already living together in an apartment in Oak Park, only ten minutes from my parents' home. I asked them if they thought asking Sarah to marry me would be too rash of a move. They said not at all. They gave me their blessing and I started looking for a ring.

I was seeking to get my spiritual house in order. I had recently been baptized by Paul Collins, a fellow waiter at the Ritz-Carlton who also ministered at Bethlehem Temple Pentecostal Church.

Paul was a righteous brother who stressed the importance of taking the plunge. It felt good to go under the water. Felt good to surrender. I relished the idea of getting my spiritual house in order. Dotting the i's and crossing the t's of my faith was important.

It also felt good to reflect on the fact that I had been baptized in a Pentecostal church, which was far closer to the heart of my grandmother than my mother. That was fine. Mom didn't mind at all. I realized that although I had disliked being dragged to church as a kid, I must have felt the spirit. The woman I called Mother had a love of God that surely touched my soul.

In fact, we went full circle when Mother, who drove from Nashville to visit us in Southfield, attended Renaissance Unity with Mom to hear me sing in the choir. Given her strict affiliation with Pentecostalism, I was surprised but glad to see her seated next to her daughter. She didn't say a word about the services. Yet when we were all leaving, Mother approached me, kissed me on the cheek, and told me she was proud.

A few years later, after my grandmother had died at age ninety-four, Mom and I had a talk. She went into a painful part of her past. It was the first time she opened up to me about being sexually harassed at the hands of the minister's son as a young girl.

"I so much wanted my mother to confront the preacher," said Mom, "and when she didn't, I assumed that I wasn't worth the bother. But then, only last month, my sister told me that our mother had, in fact, gone to the minister and told him that his son had tried to force me into sex. She read him the riot act. Had I known that—known that my mother had believed and defended me—my life would have been different. I wouldn't have carried this burden of feeling unworthy." Mom worked extra hard and accomplished a great deal to disprove that feeling of unworthiness. The attitude of feeling "less than" motivated her to prove herself. "So," she said, "I can't get angry at my mother for not telling me that she had, in fact, taken up my part. I can only be grateful that this early confusion helped me realize the need to put my spiritual house in order."

Like Mom, Sarah had her spiritual house in order. Sarah was also financially responsible. That both impressed and inspired me. Prior to Sarah, I had been getting eviction notices. I could barely pay my phone bill. Sarah, on the other hand, knew how to manage money. She walked through life with organization and ease. In the summer, she'd carefully store her winter clothes, then reverse the process when the seasons changed. Watching her efficiency edified me. I felt obligated to do the same. I saw my engagement to Sarah as essential to my maturation. It was only a question of finding the occasion to pop the question.

Mom always had big Thanksgiving dinners for the extended family. What better time to ask Sarah for her hand in marriage? I waited till the end of the evening. I almost chickened out. It was only when dinner was over and Sarah and I were walking out the door that, after helping her with her overcoat, I took out the small box and presented her with the ring. I slipped it on her finger. She smiled. She beamed. We kissed. We hugged. I didn't say a word and neither did she. I never actually popped the question. I didn't have to. Sarah understood, and so did I.

That should have been the proverbial closing of the deal, but it wasn't. Sarah presumed that it would only be a matter of time before a wedding date was set. There was a passive side to Sarah, a go-with-the-flow side, that kept her from pushing me. I appreciated that. Struggling with the proper way to put out *Kemistry*, I was grateful not to deal with other pressure.

Sarah left me alone to work out this record. She realized its significance to my life. She knew that I saw it as my future. I believe she also saw our marital union as our future.

But did I?

Yes, I gave her the ring.

Yes, I called her my fiancée.

Yes, her presence in my life was undoubtedly a blessing.

But no date was set.

I had to get back to the studio.

36

THE DETROIT HUSTLE

When I was a kid in the mid-1970s, Les McCann put out a song called "Got to Hustle to Survive." Les sang it strong. His keyboard playing was even stronger. But strongest of all was the message. I related to Les's admonition to hustle.

Once the live version of *Kemistry* was recorded, there was only one way it would survive: I had to put it out. My inability to do so goes to the heart of my musical character: I couldn't tolerate the sound. I knew the quality hadn't nearly reached its full potential. I tried rationalizing. Tried telling myself, "Given the circumstances, it's as good as it can be." But after I'd listened to it twenty or thirty times, that rationalization collapsed. I had to do better. I had to honor this suite of songs that, for better or worse, represented the longing, confusion, and faith that had brought them to life. And yet, even in this crude form, the recording brought me to an unexpected place.

———

Someone got hold of the live version and made copies. People started listening and vibing to it. They liked what they heard. I got wind of this on a Thursday night in a place called Half Past 3. Inside that downtown Detroit club was a section called the Red Room that seated a few dozen folks. Sarah was there. Her presence was always a comfort. I sat at the keyboard, hit a chord, and sang "Yesterday, I missed you sad," the opening line to "Miss You." I was shocked when suddenly everyone started singing along. It was the first time I sang one of my original, unreleased songs in front of an audience that knew every word. The melody of "Miss You" wanders. It begins out of rhythm before finding its groove. The crowd found the groove and I was transformed. I couldn't help but feel that they had also found me. Strangers were deep inside my story, to which they obviously related. We were no longer artist and audience. We were one.

It was an epiphany. Notwithstanding the fact that people were really feeling the live recording, I still felt the need to get into a studio and do the thing right. I've often joked that American Express obviously mistook me for someone else when they extended a $17,000 business line of credit to me in 2001. The truth is that, in money matters, I had been a good steward. I kept up the payments on my Amex Gold Card, which, in turn, led to the line of credit. I took the money and put it all into a studio production of what would become the *Kemistry* album.

I started working like a man possessed, first at Willray Productions, owned by Rayse Biggs, a pillar of the jazz community and later a member of my band. The work went slowly, and still something of a rookie in the studio, I was unable to get the sound I wanted. I was looking for the perfect aural blend. Unable to find it at Willray, I redoubled my efforts and entered a new phase of recording at

Masterpiece Sound, a studio belonging to Motown legend Sylvia Moy, cowriter of Stevie Wonder hits like "Uptight" and "My Cherie Amour." Engineer Carlos Gunn, one of the essential teachers in my professional life, shared my vision. My dear friend Dave McMurray, who played sax throughout the record, added just the right flavor of soulful jazz.

When I was finally satisfied, I contacted ProductionPro, a manufacturer in Chicago, and pressed up a batch of CDs. In the hopes of landing a major label, my goal was to sell ten thousand units.

The hustle was back on after initially being halted by my obsession with making *Kemistry* not simply good but great. I took years to write and record the album. I went from the live recording to driving my colleagues crazy at two different studios. Take after take after take. Mix after mix after mix.

The process was fueled by perfectionism. While I do feel that I am a perfectionist, my perfectionism, although intense, does not carry the same weight as addiction. Unlike the needy, desperate search for a high, my labor, when it comes to making music, bears results. The changes I make elevate the work. If perfectionism means improvement, then I'm all for it. Over the years I've learned how to get to what I want quicker. I've learned to step back and see the forest for the trees. No matter how you get there, at the end of the day, it's got to feel good.

Once out of the studio, I began devising an efficient financial plan. I went through Dad's stack of books on economic models. I swallowed my pride and asked for his advice. After all, this was the same guy who used to get up at four a.m. to drive me around on my *Detroit Free Press* paper route before school. After so many rough years, our relationship had evolved. He saw I was making serious progress and got behind me.

Having already found a CD manufacturer, I got a UPC code,

a graphic artist to design the package, and a techie to set up my website. I personally trekked from one independent record store to another. Fortunately, back then, indies, mom-and-pop record stores, were still plentiful. I hit up Street Corner Music in Southfield, Shantiniques in Detroit, George's Music Room in Chicago. They bought CDs from me for $10 and sold them for $15.

Unlike my mother, I've never been great at sales. It doesn't help that I'm shy. But this was different. This time I knew I had to break through my shyness. When you yourself are the product, you do what you gotta do. It was my duty to take *Kemistry* to the streets.

Mom pitched in and sold my CD along with her gift baskets and Mary Kay products. I tracked the sales at all the mom-and-pop stores we serviced. For months, I sold CDs out of the trunk of my car. The buildup was slow. When it came to figuring out the business side of things, I was no prodigy. Sometimes I waited too long to order a new batch of CDs and missed a bunch of sales. Inventory control was critical. Cash flow was even more critical. This was before YouTube viral explosions and Spotify enabled artists to avoid the traditional trek. This was old-school. One store, one disc, one listener at a time.

Some days I was hopeful. A store took a handful. Other days, when I heard "Thanks, but no thanks," I fell into despair. Who was I fooling? Folks were listening to "Bootylicious." They were buying Jamie Foxx and Alicia Keys, stars with major labels and major marketing campaigns behind them. I had Dad. I had Mom. I had Toya. God bless them all, but, for all my planning, how could I expect to gain a national audience? Detroit wasn't Atlanta or New York or LA. Detroit was still down-at-the-heels.

But I kept hearing Les McCann. The man said, "You got to hustle to survive," and the man knew what he was talking about. The Temptations said, "Ain't too proud to beg," another lesson I took to heart. So when I played the little clubs around town, I made myself say, "If you like what you hear, stop by the table at the door and pick up a CD or two. Or three. Or four. Or more. I'll be happy to sign them for you." It wasn't the best sales pitch in the world, but it was all I had.

I was encouraged when a few stores called to say they wanted five or six more CDs. Toya booked me at summer festivals—the Ribs 'n Soul Festival, the African World Festival, and TasteFest—where I would appear early in the lineup, when only a handful of spectators were present. The promoters weren't interested in me. I was just a warm-up for the headliners.

Kemistry's sales failed to soar on a national level, but locally we were heating up. In the big scheme of things, it was a slow build. Which was fitting because, looking back, I see everything in my life as a slow build. Yet a slow build in sales meant that I couldn't become a full-time artist. I needed to hold on to my job at the Ritz-Carlton, which often meant working nights. On one such night, I was set to serve at a big banquet. It was a night when I was convinced that I was in the right place at the right time.

37

ALIGNING OF THE STARS

I had a feeling something extraordinary was in the air even before I got to my Saturday-night gig at the Ritz-Carlton. That feeling was confirmed when I looked at the banquet's program. I was blown away to see that the host, General Motors, had hired a super band to entertain its guests that night. David Sanborn on sax. Joe Sample and George Duke on keys. Vocals by Roberta Flack. And Al Jarreau! I could hardly contain myself. The timing was perfect. These were the people I was meant to meet, the musicians who could help take me to the next level. I always carried a couple of copies of the *Kemistry* CD with me and was convinced that George Duke, a prolific and stellar producer, would dig it. Not to mention Al Jarreau.

When I saw the band coming in for sound check, I made my move. I wandered around the back of the stage and spotted Al. I can be easily intimidated, but this time I couldn't stay away. Besides, Al seemed approachable. I introduced myself and told him how much his version of "Blue in Green" meant to me.

"Oh, man," he said, "it means just as much for me to hear you say that."

Al spoke like he sang, in sudden bursts of joy. His spirit was filled with spontaneous wonder and surprise. He took his time to explain how the song reflected the relationship between Miles Davis and arranger Gil Evans. How they heard each other so clearly. He talked about the love and appreciation they shared. The way Gil challenged Miles and the way Miles responded to the challenge. The way Al, in singing this song, felt obliged to challenge himself. He spoke at length, and he spoke generously. His humility was profound.

"Miles and Gil are in a class all their own," he said. "I don't put myself up there with them. I don't put myself down, but I can't help but be grateful that great artists like them can raise the sights of a guy like me."

I did put Al in the Miles Davis/Gil Evans category, and I wanted to tell him just that. Instead, I merely said that I, too, loved albums like *Miles Ahead* and *Sketches of Spain*. I, too, was inspired.

When Al indicated he had to run, a strange thing happened. Despite my plan to slip him a copy of *Kemistry*, I surprised myself by backing off. The beauty of our conversation stopped me. I didn't want it to end with a hustle. I wanted to keep it pure.

"I love your music, Al Jarreau," I said. "And I always will."

He smiled, gave me a hug, and was on his way. I'd been blessed.

At the evening's end, after the food was served and the band had performed, I shifted back into hustle mode. I saw George Duke about to head out the door and, just in time, caught his attention. I knew, of course, that George and Al had a long history that had begun during the Haight-Ashbury Summer of Love in San Francisco when they were playing jazz standards while Jefferson Airplane was playing psychedelic rock. Since then, George had expanded as a producer for everyone from Taste of Honey to Barry Manilow. If anyone could get me a deal, it was George. If only he'd listen to *Kemistry*. I asked him to do so.

"Wish I could," he said in a friendly voice, "but I have this policy of not accepting any music on the road. Let me give you my office address in LA. Just send it there and I'll give it a listen. Wish I could stop now, but we're on our way to the airport."

George wrote out the address on a card and handed it to me.

"I wish you all the best, man," he said. "God bless."

A great cat, but also a super-busy cat. I understood. I took the card and thanked him. I never did send the CD. I figured it'd only get lost in the shuffle.

Reflecting on the evening's series of events, I was convinced it was all divine timing. I believe it was God's will that I meet Al and encounter George. At the time, I might not have gotten what I wanted—a quick passport to success—but I got what I needed: a chance to speak with one of my heroes and a mandate to be patient.

38

DREAMING ON BROADWAY

The Ritz-Carlton had helped me in countless ways. But being there was holding me back. Though I needed the income, I'd find a way to make it. And making it meant devoting all of my time to promoting *Kemistry*.

It wasn't an easy decision, and the meeting with the hotel HR director was tough. She was a lovely woman who knew about my music ambitions. A music fan herself, she was never discouraging. But she was practical. As an act of kindness, she suggested that I give the standard two weeks' notice. That would allow me a safety net to come back into the fold if things didn't work out. I thanked her but said I didn't need a safety net. I could always get another job waiting tables. I needed the fear of stepping out into the unknown to fuel my motivation.

So, back to the grind. Always back to the grind. Back to the indie stores, back to the summer festivals, back to the small clubs, back to Mom's selling my CDs to her clients, Dad's helping me figure out the financials, and my trying to figure out my relationship with Sarah. Sarah, whom I loved. Sarah, who loved me. Sarah, whose positive energy had galvanized mine. Sarah, who disagreed with a friend claiming my ambition to sell ten thousand CDs was unrealistic. Sarah, who said, "You'll sell even more."

Sarah was right. We sold seventeen thousand. Sarah, who was the first person I called when Toya gave me the news: Not only were major labels interested in picking up *Kemistry*, but the label showing the most interest was Motown, the same Motown that symbolized the aspirational energy of the city I called my own, the city that seemed, against all odds, to be propping me up. I looked back and saw that during the 1967 summer of my birth, Motown's smash hits were Marvin Gaye and Tammi Terrell singing "Ain't No Mountain High Enough," and Smokey Robinson and the Miracles begging for "more love," the love coming my way from places totally unexpected. Didn't that have to be God's will?

Maybe, maybe not. Motown boss Kedar Massenburg had sent for me to play a couple of songs for him in their New York office, but nothing was for certain. Maybe he'd like my live performance; maybe he wouldn't. I had to calm myself down. I couldn't get ahead of myself. By the time I came along, Motown was a long way from the mean streets of Detroit. Motown lived in a midtown Manhattan skyscraper and its big stars were Brian McKnight, Erykah Badu, and India Arie. The term *neo-soul* was being bandied about, a designation that, as far as I could see, did not apply to me. Any notion that I was mystically connected to the great Motown lineage was a pipe dream.

At the same time, corporations respect numbers, and Universal, Motown's parent company, had seen that I had, in fact, sold seventeen thousand CDs on my own. Massenburg heard *Kemistry* and liked it, but before he committed he wanted to see me perform under pressure. He was willing to gamble the price of a trip to New York for me, my three-piece band, and my sound man.

Sitting up in my New York hotel room the night before, I listened to George Benson's "On Broadway." Maybe my song choice was a bit obvious—the hotel was on Broadway. I was trying to take it all in. "On Broadway" was the first song I sang live when I was a kid, and I would be walking up to Motown's office the next morning, which was on Broadway. The lyrics talked about the neon lights' being bright, the same garish pink and green lights shining through the curtains of my room. The message of the song goes into the story of an artist who's come to conquer Broadway, who won't quit till he becomes a star. The song always brought me back to an earlier era before I was born, to the 1960s, when the song was written by Broadway Brill Building writers Barry Mann, Cynthia Weil, Jerry Leiber, and Mike Stoller and sung by the Drifters, whose old records I had heard when I was a child back in Pontiac. Maybe I was excited to be part of a tradition of great blues-based music, or maybe I was excited to add my own flavor to that tradition, or maybe it was just the honking horns of the midnight taxis that kept me up all night, or the idea that tomorrow I'd be auditioning, like the singer of the song, "on Broadway," for a chance to finally get where I wanted to go.

That night I slipped in and out of dreams. I had sprouted wings and was soaring like an eagle. I was driving a Ferrari through the Painted Desert. I was swimming with dolphins and riding rockets to Mars. The dreams collided.

The neon lights outside my hotel room faded into dawn. The morning light was harsh. A shower helped ease my nerves. I dressed in a pin-striped suit and an open-necked black shirt. Black Ferragamo shoes. Heavy-framed tinted glasses. I felt cool except for the fact that I was lugging my big keyboard case four blocks up Broadway to the Motown office. The band met me an hour before the meeting. They put us in a room where a neon sign over a small stage read, "Motown-Universal Welcomes KEM." Sound check. There was a tune-up and a last remark from my manager Toya.

"What Motown is really saying to you is, 'Kem, all this hype we've heard about you better be true. You better be worth the bread we've spent bringing you here. You better knock us out or, if not, go back to Detroit and keep selling CDs out of the trunk of your car.'"

The room was starting to feel warm. I was starting to feel claustrophobic. But the moment Kedar Massenburg entered the room accompanied by sibling music executives Monte and Avery Lipman, I shook it off. Their greeting was warm. I felt that they were rooting for me. I felt the adrenaline coursing through my veins, but I was steady. I said, "Thanks for inviting us. If you're ready, we are."

It only took two songs. In fact, all they wanted was two songs. The first had to be "Matter of Time," because it was time. And the second had to be "Love Calls," because that was the album cut getting the most attention. Love did call. Love had prevailed during thousands of hours sitting at the keyboard constructing thousands of configurations until they fell together and made sense of a mystery that would never be solved but, if sung honestly, might touch the human heart.

When I was through singing the songs, the applause was immediate. So were Massenburg's words. "There's no gimmick with you, man," he said. "You're a true artist. You're essentially a guy who walked in, sat at the keyboard, and sang the hell out of his songs."

The deal was done. Motown offered me a multialbum contract. Over a month's time, my attorney worked on the details. All parties were satisfied. Then came the day of days. The day of signing. I should have been thrilled. Instead, I fell apart.

39

BREAKDOWN

Just when you're breaking down, you may well be breaking through. The problem is you don't know that in real time, while it's happening. All you know is that you're falling apart. And in the process, despair has replaced hope. You're wiped out.

Ironically, the opposite happened to me. Just when I had won—just when my breakthrough was documented in the form of a recording contract—I broke down. I couldn't sign it. Didn't even want to look at it. Didn't want to think about it. Wanted to run and hide.

Why? It didn't make any sense. This was what I'd been working for. Years of struggle had finally paid off. Circumstances had conspired to give me exactly what I wanted. But there I was, up at three a.m., my brain on fire with a fear I couldn't even name. I was in bed with Sarah. We were engaged to be married. Seemingly, my personal life was in order. Motown's offer should have meant my professional life was in order. Yet my mind was spinning. I felt like I was going crazy.

I got out of bed and walked into the kitchen. I started pacing like a tiger in a cage. I felt trapped. What was the cage? Nothing but a metaphor. A figment of my imagination. The only cage was a mental cage. I wanted to wish it away, the way you shake yourself awake after a bad dream. But I couldn't. I kept turning the lights on and off. I managed to get from the kitchen to the living room. Tried to sit down. Couldn't stay down. Thought of walking outside but it was the dead of night. It was cold. I needed to stay inside. Needed to get back in bed with Sarah. Fall asleep. Get a good night's rest. Everything would be all right in the morning. In my mind's eye, I saw the contract. It was downstairs on my desk waiting to be signed. My lawyer said it was fair. The only thing left was to just lock it in. Let Motown take over sales. National distribution. National marketing. All good. Then why did I see this contract as a death warrant? I couldn't sign off on my death warrant. I could feel my brain spiraling out of control. Sarah was fast asleep and waking her would be unfair. Same for Toya. Besides, Toya would be justifiably adamant. She'd tell me to just sign the damn thing. Mom knew me better than anyone. Mom would understand.

Because she had experienced the same sort of trauma, when I called my mom, she knew I was having a panic attack. I couldn't focus. I was breathing heavily. I couldn't keep still. I didn't have the language to articulate how I was feeling. I just knew something was fundamentally wrong. I was sure something was physically wrong with me. That was my immediate concern. Had I suffered a stroke? Was I losing my mind?

Thank God for Mom's practicality. She simply said, "Have Sarah take you to the ER. I'll meet you there."

An hour later, the ER doctor said, "Your vitals are fine. I'll give you something to help you sleep when you get home, but I'd strongly recommend you see a psychiatrist. This is a mental issue."

Mental issue? Was I being called a mental case? I didn't argue because, on the face of it, I *was* a mental case. The facts were plain: In the face of being offered everything I wanted, I was freaking out. I'd experienced a full-blown meltdown.

Back home, I took the pill and finally slept. I woke up in the early afternoon feeling disoriented. I thought of praying but I couldn't. I felt completely estranged from any spiritual awareness. I was falling into a hole of deep depression. If I was so close to God, how could this be happening? And if God was just an illusion, where did that leave me?

Meanwhile, the contract remained unsigned.

Pressure was building. Toya, who had worked tirelessly to get me this deal, was not happy. Neither was my lawyer. Motown, who had given me creative freedom, didn't understand the delay.

I knew that the problem was psychological. Even though I come from a culture and a generation that traditionally resists seeking the counsel of shrinks, I was desperate to learn what was going on. On the surface, it made no sense. A long-term breakdown would derail my career at the very moment when it was taking off. I had to be honest with myself: mentally, I was a mess.

I went to Renaissance Unity that Sunday. I needed quietude and prayer. I wasn't up to singing in the choir, but after services I saw one of the female singers who had become a close friend. She saw the anxiety in my eyes. She asked if anything was wrong. I gave her a brief description of what I was experiencing. She said it sounded like I was suffering from depression—clinical depression. I tried to hide my astonishment at hearing those words. She comforted me and mentioned that she had a close colleague who was a psychiatrist. She asked if I wanted the doctor's name and number. I hesitated before saying yes.

40

BREAKTHROUGH

I called Monday morning and saw her that afternoon. I didn't deliberately seek a woman of color but was not displeased when that was what she turned out to be. She was Indian. She was soft-spoken, empathetic, and smart. Her degrees, all from prestigious institutions of higher learning, hung on a wall behind her desk. In front of her desk were two club chairs, each with a footstool. We sat facing one another.

Earlier, I had asked the hospital to send her the ER report. She read it over carefully and asked how I was doing. Not great, I said. She wanted me to elaborate. This was my first time seeing a psychiatrist, so verbal elaboration did not come easily. A twelve-step program is one thing. A fellowship is assumed. Over time, intimacy grows. But this medical doctor specializing in mental issues was something altogether different. My default position—silence—was kicking in. My nonresponse, though, didn't bother her. I'm sure she was used to it. Gently, she pushed me to reveal what was happening in my life. Hesitantly, I told her about the long gestation period leading to the birth of *Kemistry* and the current Motown offer.

She understood. She saw that I was starting a new and exciting chapter in my life. But then she said something that caught my attention. She said this was a chapter I couldn't control.

She wasn't wrong. She went on to say that until now, I had tightly controlled the project. She knew the project was dear to my heart. But now that it was about to be released to the world, that release was no longer under my auspices. A corporation was taking over. And that idea was frightening.

I asked whether I was wrong to be frightened. She answered that right and wrong weren't the point. The point was to address my fear and not to judge it.

I felt that the fear was flipping me out.

The doctor didn't see it that way. She agreed that I seemed on edge. But no, she didn't see me flipping out. She saw someone sitting across from her trying to deal with tremendous stress.

I confessed that I'd also been withdrawn. I hadn't wanted to talk to anyone. I'd been depressed. Fear and depression, she said, were first cousins. Their relationship was in the blood. Their intensity also relates to self-esteem. She wondered about the state of my self-esteem. I pointed out that it should have been at its highest level. The Motown deal was the ultimate validation.

There's a difference between "should be" and "is." The psychiatrist saw outside validation as a good thing but not a permanent phenomenon. For a feeling of self-worth to last, it must come from within. I was about to step onto a national stage. That meant I'd be more vulnerable than ever. That also meant that I was seeking a new level of validation.

I wondered if I was wrong to seek that validation.

The doctor didn't think so. She could see that part of me was confident; without confidence, I couldn't have gotten where I was. But there was another part of me that feared failure. That part had been triggered and thrown me into this crisis.

The negative voices, as always, sparked up again, *Okay, some people are buying your music, but your music is hardly mainstream. You'll never be Michael Jackson or Prince or Usher. You'll never be Luther. You'll never play—never mind sell out—Madison Square Garden. All you've got is these quiet little songs at a time when quiet little songs are hardly in vogue. 50 Cent's* Get Rich or Die Tryin' *is taking the world by storm. Your music is a million miles away from that. You're going from a little pond out into the vast ocean. Chances are, you'll drown.*

Yet, paradoxically, when the doctor asked me if I was afraid that, in the hands of Motown, *Kemistry* would fail, I had another answer: I was also afraid the record would succeed! And if it did succeed, my songs would be in the hands of a marketing machine. I'd lose control of my music. I'd lose control of my career. I was afraid of losing control of my life altogether. If I didn't sign the contract, I wouldn't run that risk. But not to sign would be idiotic.

She said that I wouldn't be the first person who, during a moment of uncertainty and fear, chose to self-sabotage.

I wanted to know how to avoid the self-sabotage. Her advice was to see the conflict for what it was. And what was it? Her three-word reply hit home: the human condition.

I let out a huge sigh. I knew the doctor was right. One part of me was raring to conquer the world. Another part of me wanted to go home and hide. And still another part was ashamed of wanting to go home and hide. I admitted all this. She referred to my ongoing participation in twelve-step groups. She presumed that, in my experience, the idea of harsh self-negation was not new. It wasn't.

The doctor was quick to say that negative self-image, especially when it starts at an early age, does not easily dissolve. It stays. I sighed another big sigh. It was a lot to take in.

She reminded me, though, that I was, in fact, taking it in. I wasn't running from this session. I wasn't resisting. I wasn't afraid to look inside.

But I was afraid that my anxiety and depression might get worse. If so, what was I supposed to do?

She recommended a psychotropic drug that might help. Was I willing?

I was willing to consider it.

Before the session ended, she wanted to know how I felt about what we had discussed. I admitted that I was a little confused, but I did feel a little hopeful. When she heard the word *hopeful*, she broke into a smile.

41

THE TAKEOFF

I have friends who are afraid of flying. I feel for them. You get into a massive hunk of metal machinery that you don't understand or command. You don't know why it's able to fly through the sky without crashing to the ground. You obsess about the crash. You're convinced that your number is up. You're consumed with fear.

I was feeling something like that when I officially turned *Kemistry* over to Motown. I didn't understand their marketing strategy or how they would position me. Hell, I didn't even know what a marketing strategy was. But most of all, I didn't know what would be required of me on this new level. I didn't know if I was up for the challenge. I wasn't red-carpet material. I didn't relish the idea of being a celebrity and doing the celebrity dance. I was too grounded for that. I was too in touch with my humble beginnings, and I wanted to keep it that way. It made me feel safe.

The psychiatrist helped me see that my depression and anxiety weren't just about getting a record deal and fearing that my music wouldn't be accepted by a mainstream audience. They were also about finally seizing the brass ring after all these years and realizing that success wouldn't heal my ambivalence over my relationship with Sarah, to whom I still could not commit. Neither would it heal the heartache of never knowing my real dad. I was terrified and on the brink of a nervous breakdown. To control that terror, I agreed to take an antidepressant. It helped. It may well have saved me from what the doctor had called self-sabotage. I was able to sign the contract. I did so with a mixture of relief and trepidation. I knew I'd been paralyzed by fear. My signature released the paralysis but not the apprehension. My stomach was still in knots.

The knots loosened when I saw Motown pick up the project where I had left off. If I had been moving at ten miles per hour, Motown put the pedal to the metal and goosed it up to a hundred miles per hour. They were able to service radio in a way that I and my homegrown team could never have imagined. Universal's distribution component was exactly what was needed—not to mention the advertising and special appearances arranged for me. Suddenly, *Kemistry* was selling six thousand copies a week. And that went on for weeks. Sixteen months later, it would be certified gold, with sales over a half million. I was baffled, thrilled, dizzy, even giddy on the inside, but outwardly I remained cool. I did my best to stay centered.

My band was anchored by Dave McMurray. Among all my original players, including myself, he had the most experience as a professional musician. We all found ourselves following his lead when it came to song arrangements, set list management, and handling yourself on the road. I was far from the best musician onstage. I had enough spiritual grounding to avoid ego tripping. At least that's what I told myself. Rather than cloak myself in glory, I could give God the glory. And I did so. During my concerts, I testified about my belief in the power of God's love and its ability to transform our lives. That love informs my music. Because I was moving into my midthirties, I had a maturity that I had sorely lacked a decade earlier. Had I achieved stardom in, say, my early twenties, I would have undercut it. Like cocaine, celebrity is heady stuff. Also like cocaine, celebrity cranks up the ego to the point of implosion. They both—fame and coke—can separate you from your soul.

But having maintained my sobriety for a dozen years, having walked through this recent anxiety attack, and having maintained my close relationship to the church Mom had led me to, I should have been able to easily glide through this initiation into the culture of celebrity.

I'm afraid that I did not glide. I stumbled, and, I am not happy to report, I hurt people in the process.

42

DOUBLE DEALING

My relationship with Sarah was never superficial. Our emotional bond was deep. I helped her through the grief she suffered when her mother died. She helped me through the birth of *Kemistry*. On evenings out, we heard great music. On Sundays we would visit one of our favorite restaurants, Beans & Cornbread over on Northwestern Highway. Seated in the audience, I was proud to see Sarah take her law degree. When her close friend graduated from Middle Tennessee State University in Murfreesboro, I accompanied her to the ceremony.

But what about our ceremony? Our wedding? That was the elephant in the room. The racial aspect of marrying a white woman was always there. A Black woman who sang in the Renaissance Unity choir with me once said derisively, "Why are you with that white woman?"

My answers—"Because she's my fiancée" and "Because I love

her"—didn't satisfy my inquisitor. That night when I mentioned the incident to Sarah, she wondered whether I was ashamed of the fact that we were together. Maybe I was. And to make matters worse, maybe I was ashamed of being ashamed. Double shame is a killer.

Whatever my emotional confusion, I continued to avoid the ultimate act. No wedding date, no invitations, no commitment.

One weekend I opened for Rachelle Ferrell at the State Theater in Detroit. Rachelle is a master vocalist who seamlessly combines the same genres I seek to solidify in my work. I can listen to her sing all day. That night she performed flawlessly. Afterward, I sought some face time with her, simply to tell her how much I admired her. Sarah had come with a friend but would be riding home with me after the show. She stood in the wings waiting for me. I could have invited her over and introduced her to Rachelle. I could have said, "Meet my fiancée." Or "Meet my girlfriend." But I did neither. I pretended not to see Sarah standing off in the distance. Perturbed, she walked off while I chatted with Rachelle. Sarah never mentioned what I had done, but I knew she was upset. She didn't like confrontations and neither did I. So, I reverted to silence.

My silence spoke volumes. Sarah sensed that I was withdrawing. At the same time, *Kemistry* was taking off, and I was in a whirlwind of touring and publicity and personal appearances. Yet I managed to become drawn to Emily Daniel, whose family I'd known from Renaissance Unity for several years. I was instrumental in getting Emily's mother into the choir. Emily would eventually sing in the choir as well.

Emily had a sparkling personality. A voracious reader, she was intense, precocious, talented, ambitious, and also white. She was a doe-eyed brunette with a great figure. She was another natural beauty. She was also a searcher, a petite force of boundless energy.

I discussed the dilemma with my psychiatrist, always an insightful listener. After going on and on about how I didn't want to betray Sarah and yet I was strongly attracted to Emily, the doctor stopped me.

She said I was going around and around, trying to justify something I'd already made up my mind to do. She saw a dalliance with Emily as my way of distancing myself from Sarah. I started to argue. I didn't like having my mind read. But when I flew Emily from Detroit to New Orleans, where I was performing one weekend, I had to admit that the doctor had, in fact, read my mind.

I kept my involvement with Emily secret because I was not willing to either honor my commitment to Sarah or end it. My equivocation with Sarah had been going on for years. I can't say that both women were willing to go along with my infidelity. But they were aware of one another and both were hopeful I would come to my senses.

One night, after doing a show, I was in a hotel in Chicago with Sarah. The phone rang. I quickly picked it up and heard Emily's voice. I said a few words and hung up as though it were nothing.

"Was that her?" asked Sarah.

The question startled me. "No," I lied.

A few weeks later, I asked Sarah if any of her friends knew I'd been unfaithful. She said yes. Were they surprised? I asked.

"No," she replied, "but they *are* surprised that you're unwilling to try to work it out."

Sarah knew several couples who had benefited from counseling. And because I was already seeing a psychiatrist, I assumed she had hoped I'd be open to couples therapy. I wasn't. I felt like I'd broken her heart.

I was then—and am now—ashamed of my hypocrisy. It was especially terrible because I continued to speak, both in church and in concert, about my recovery and my faith. On that score, I wasn't lying. I was free from alcohol and drugs. I was sober. I tithed. I testified. At the same time, I was a romantic mess. My messiness was rooted in fear. I was afraid of marrying Sarah in part because I thought it would have a negative impact on my career. Starting off as a new artist in your thirties is tough enough. Why make it tougher by walking down the aisle with a white woman? I was serious about my career. I still am. At this early juncture I was wary of making the wrong move.

On a deeper level, my concern for my career was only a cover for the real reason I didn't want to marry Sarah. I did love Sarah, but I suspect if my love had been all-consuming, it would have assuaged all my concerns. But my love for Sarah, no matter how genuine, had limits. Those limits marked its demise.

For months, I led a double life, or even a triple life. One with Sarah, another with Emily, and a third public life as an emerging artist singing about the urgency of love. I was all over the place and seemingly unable to commit to or quit either woman.

Sarah fed into my sense of mature and stable love; Emily represented romantic intrigue. I wanted both. I wanted everything. *Kemistry* continued to build. I was traveling, making it easier to postpone decisions. I was purposely derailing my relationship with Sarah by having an affair with Emily, all the while writing what would become *Kem: Album II*.

43

SUCCESS AND SOLITUDE

Being an artist, especially an R & B artist, means being in show business. And show business, for all its glitz and glamour, is a monster that, unless you're exceedingly careful, can eat you alive.

I was lucky. I didn't gain full entry into the heady world of show business until I was thirty-six. By then I was hardly a starry-eyed kid. I was also lucky that I had tied my faith to a paradigm, a twelve-step program whose loving ethos was rooted in the soil of pure Christianity. Staying close to those roots kept me from relapsing. Once I was sober, the temptation to drug and drink was no longer there—not because it magically disappeared but because I stayed in the program.

I want to use the word *temperance* because it seems best suited to describe my state as a newly minted celebrity, but temperance is associated with self-restraint, self-control, moderation—so I'm a little reluctant to do so. In matters of money, I did display restraint.

But in other areas, like emotional commitment, I can claim no success. I still didn't know how to deal with romance or, for that matter, understand what romance was all about. Coming from a writer of romantic songs, that's an uncomfortable confession. When it came to women, I was still tripping.

When it came to finances, I was not. In the first flush of national success, I did not buy a Rolls. I bought a used 2001 Toyota Avalon. I didn't buy a splashy pad in Beverly Hills. I did not mistake myself for a crossover pop star. I was, in fact, an adult artist whose audience consisted of grown folks who had profound knowledge of and respect for the musical tradition from which I'd emerged. As time went on, that audience also knew that my spoken testimony of God's grace was as important to me as the music. Whether that limited or expanded my popularity wasn't of concern to me. It was something I simply needed to express.

I remained low-key. I stayed put in metropolitan Detroit. In an instance where my father's sense of frugality was of great benefit, he found me a reasonably priced single-story ranch-style home in Lathrup Village, a quiet community not far from where Mom had moved us after she hit the number. I loved that house. I still do. From time to time, I still work in its homemade studio.

I lived in that house alone. I protected, even relished, my solitude because I knew solitude was a necessary part of my creative process. I didn't write songs spontaneously at parties or while I was out on the road traveling between shows. I wrote them at home—alone.

Sarah did not move in with me. Neither did Emily. The most frequent guests were my mother, my father, and my daughter, Troi. My house became my refuge. My house became a character in my life whose purpose was to center me so, undisturbed, I could focus on work. The street was quiet. The front and back yards were nicely manicured. The interior was just spacious enough. Three bedrooms, two baths, a living room, a dining room, a kitchen. And, much to my delight, a basement, a hideaway, where I could set up my gear and work to my heart's content. That house demanded nothing from me. The mortgage payment was manageable. A million houses in suburban America look just like it. Yet, at that point in my life, it was special. It spoke to me. It said, "Come in. Live here. Work here. This is where you can get yourself together."

Well, I did and I didn't.

Kedar Massenburg had been replaced by Sylvia Rhone, a Black woman who had worked her way up the ranks to become the head of Motown and one of the most skilled music execs in the game. There was mutual respect between us but never a close personal relationship. That was hardly Sylvia's fault. Other artists are adept at cultivating genuine friendships with their corporate counterparts. I'd be a fool not to see that as an integral part of doing good business. I'm just not very adept at it.

No drinking, no smoking, no late-night hangs. I could have been characterized as an introvert masquerading as an extrovert. If the label requested my attendance at a corporate event, I'd go. I'd even entertain. But the minute I was offstage, I was gone. Pressing the flesh and socializing are not my strong suits. I just wanted to get back to my solitude, my house in Lathrup Village, where I could sit at the keyboard and lose myself in sound.

After *Kemistry*, my emotional chemistry changed. I was a man dealing with two women, both sharp, both loving, both devoted to me. But I lacked the emotional intelligence and integrity to be honest with myself about these relationships—and consequently I couldn't be honest with them.

How could I reconcile my integrity as an artist with my integrity as a man?

44

FIND YOUR WAY

Kem: *Album II* was released in 2005. I had turned thirty-eight and, more than ever, was deep into writing, recording, and touring. If you called me a careerist, I wouldn't argue. I'd found what I loved doing most and wanted to do nothing else.

In this early stage, my performances were modestly arranged. I mostly sang at the keyboard and tried to re-create the intimacy of my recordings.

At the same time, I value privacy. Once offstage, I'm happy, even eager, to remain unnoticed. I remember feeling that way when, the day after a show, I arrived at Chicago's O'Hare to fly home. I was comforted by my anonymity. Walking through the airport, I saw one of my favorite singers, Dennis Edwards, the man who had replaced David Ruffin as lead singer in the Temptations. He was the voice of, among other huge hits, "Papa Was a Rollin' Stone" and "I Can't Get Next to You." He was surrounded by an entourage. He wore a glittery suit that sparkled under the fluorescent lights. As he passed me by, I turned around and saw that across the back of his jacket, in big glossy gold letters, were written the words *DENNIS EDWARDS*. I smiled. Not everyone could pull that off. I sure couldn't. Witnessing that display made me more mindful of the split deep inside my soul: I wanted maximum attention as an artist, while as a person wandering through airports, I relished being left alone.

By the time I started *Kem: Album II*, Sarah and I had broken up. There were no public scenes, no screaming, no drama. Sarah was a lady and I tried to be a gentleman. I use the word *gentleman* hesitantly. After it was clear that I could not honor our engagement, I did make it plain that she could always call on me for help. But Sarah didn't need my help.

For more than a decade, Emily and I would maintain our relationship, although it was always a roller-coaster ride. There were times when we were close; times when we drifted in different directions; times when we thought it was over, only to learn it wasn't. Just as I could never commit to Sarah, the same was true with Emily. And just as Sarah had tolerated my equivocation, Emily did the same. Our relationship was always under a cloud.

Working on *Kem: Album II*, I began as I've always begun—on an electric keyboard. I longed for a Steinway grand, but my father's lessons on fiscal responsibility still held. A Steinway grand costs a fortune. However, I did end up replacing my beloved Ensoniq MR76 keyboard with a Yamaha Motif. And the search for the lost chords began anew. I needed those chords because chords carry spirit. The initial spirit of a song is wordless. When the cluster of notes begins to feel right, I find myself humming, mumbling, scatting, uttering nonsense noises that, without forethought, turn into phrases. I do so without prior intention. It just happens.

One of the first songs to emerge for the new album reflected my romantic struggles. I called it "Find Your Way (Back in My Life)."

Just when I thought my relationship with Emily had come to an end, I found myself back in her arms. The initial inspiration of a song, though, has a way of morphing itself into a myriad of alternate interpretations. For example, this story could apply to Sarah. In fact, it could apply to an untold number of romantic relationships that have nothing to do with me, relationships caught up in endless turmoil that defy a definitive ending but instead linger like daydreams. You try your best to end them, but they have a mind—and a heart—all their own.

Much to my delight, I quickly learned that sometimes songs impact the listener more than the writer. That was true of "Find Your Way." Friends and fans kept telling me how they personally related to the story. In fact, they took it to be *their* story. I loved hearing that. Released from my heart, the feelings landed in the grooves of other people's lives.

The obvious became clear: writing about myself was the same as writing about others. When my music went out in the world, it no longer belonged to me. It belonged to the listener. And people were free to make of it whatever they liked. If it became someone's story—even while it was also mine—I was doubly blessed.

Maybe even triply blessed, because the song from *Kem: Album II* that exploded came about despite one of my most blatant character defects: pride.

45

THE HAT

Historically, brothers are known to love hats, and I can attest that I'm no different. But because I have a small head, I've rarely found a lid that suits me just so. I did, however, end up finding one that fit perfectly. In my mind it gave me a very subtle but distinct swag. Designed by Dolce & Gabbana, it was a knitted black wool bucket-style hat. It was as soft as cashmere. The turned-down wraparound lid stopped just above my eyebrows. Snug against my skin, it made me feel secure. I loved it to death.

I was wearing it when I flew from Detroit to New York to mix the single of a song Motown saw as a smash, "I Can't Stop Loving You." It was another one of those stories that could apply to Sarah or Emily or even God. The label was convinced it was the perfect follow-up to "Love Calls," my first number one record. Sylvia Rhone had called me herself to check on my progress with my sophomore effort and was excited about releasing the new single.

A Lincoln Town Car picked me up at LaGuardia Airport. The plan was to check into the Hilton, get a good night's sleep, and in the morning head down to Sterling Sound in lower Manhattan to master the record. Everything was lining up. The ride to the city was pleasant. I couldn't help but be pleased that "Brotha Man," a song off the *Kemistry* album, was playing on the radio. Other singers might have told the driver, "Hey, that's me." But, as you know by now, that's not my style. It was enough to just sit back and take it in.

When we pulled up to the Hilton, I grabbed my bags and headed inside. But before I reached the front door, I realized that I'd left my beloved Dolce & Gabbana bucket hat on the backseat. Like a rocket, I ran after the car. But which car? Every other car was a black Lincoln Town Car just like the one I had ridden in. No matter; I trotted alongside of as many of them as I could, trying to get a peek at the driver. Racing down Avenue of the Americas, stopping every black Lincoln Town Car I could, I failed miserably. My driver was gone. My hat was gone. My security blanket was gone. I was crushed.

I ran over to Bloomingdale's and Saks Fifth Avenue to see if they had a sufficient substitute for the hat I loved so dearly. They did not. Other models didn't work. The wool was scratchy, or the shape didn't fit my face. I gave up. Despondent, I took a cab downtown to Sterling Sound to master the record. But when I got there, the place was empty. Without my knowing, the session had been canceled. I called Toya to find out what had happened. She said I needed to head to Sylvia's office right away.

Hatless and half furious, I made the trip back to midtown. The traffic was crazy. The crawl was endless. Cars and limos rushing people to the theater district had Times Square gridlocked. I was not a happy camper.

When I finally got to Sylvia's office, she came right to the point.

She had canceled the mastering session because she wanted me to redo the ending of the song. She said that it didn't reach an emotional peak. She felt that I needed to add background harmonies or ad-libs, something to lift the energy of the record and close it out strong.

I reminded her that, as recently as yesterday, she had thought it was fine. She had given her approval. That's why I'd rushed to New York to mix and master.

She reminded me that people can change their minds. And obviously she had changed hers. After listening to it several more times, she was certain I could do a better job. She wanted me to return to the studio and record additional vocals.

I respected that Sylvia Rhone had gotten to the top of the game. I respected her experience and her taste. It was Sylvia who hooked me up with mixing engineer Ray Bardani, famous for his work with Luther Vandross. Ray would upgrade my sound for years to come. Sylvia knew what she was doing. But I still hated the idea of revamping a strong song that I was sure was fine as is.

When I asked how she could justify this last-minute maneuver, she just shrugged her shoulders, as if to say, "I'm the boss. I don't need to justify shit."

She wanted me to get back to the studio and record that very night. I refused. I told her I was going home. I was pissed. And she didn't care. Meeting over.

I felt disheveled. Discouraged. This trip to New York, not the easiest city to navigate, had been a bust. Ever since I'd lost that damn hat, everything had gone wrong. I gave a deep sigh, went back to the Hilton, and fell into an uneasy sleep.

Next morning, I took another black Lincoln Town Car to La-Guardia, still debating whether Sylvia was right to insist that I redo the vocals.

When I got to the Delta terminal, I grabbed my bag and headed inside. Before I reached the door, I heard a car come to a screeching halt. Someone had gotten out and yelled, "Hey, sir! Sir! Sir! I have your hat." I turned to see that it was the driver who had originally picked me up from the airport a few days prior.

I ran over. He handed me the Dolce & Gabbana black knitted bucket hat. I thanked him profusely, tipped him twenty bucks, and put it on my head. I felt like a new man. More than that, I felt blessed. In that moment God's hand on my life was reaffirmed. As if he was saying, "I know you are disappointed. I know you are hurt. But I've still got you."

Two days later, back in Detroit, I capitulated. I went over to Masterpiece Sound and cut the additional background vocals and ad-libs. I sat back and listened. Sylvia was right.

When "I Can't Stop Loving You" was released, it soared to number one, becoming the biggest-selling single of my career. It became, in fact, a signature song.

For the first interview to promote the single at a Detroit radio station, I wore a black Adidas tracksuit and fresh Prada sneakers, topped off by—you guessed it—my D & G bucket hat.

46

EASY BREEZY

My early shows were not extravagant. When it came to stage presentation, I was inexperienced. I was far more focused on the music than, say, the way I looked. I stayed seated at the electric keyboard, not because I was afraid to stand up and sing, but because I didn't trust anyone else to accompany me the way I wanted to be accompanied. The songs I had written for the first two albums, all keyboard based, were woven around subtle inversions peculiar to me. The only other guy who could have given me the necessary support was Brian O'Neal, my friend from high school, who long ago had relocated to Atlanta.

My fashion style, like my keyboard style, was far from showy. My go-to outfit for a show was linen drawstring slacks and a crisp white shirt. I wore loafers without socks and even flip-flops. In the wintertime, I was partial to cream-colored turtlenecks and pale blue V-neck sweaters. It wasn't complicated.

Unfortunately, I couldn't say the same thing about my ongoing relationship with Emily. For long periods of time, we could relax in one another's company. Emily, who had worked with future presidential aspirant Marianne Williamson, was intellectually astute. While I was on the keyboard for hours on end, she was stretched out on the couch, deep into Paulo Coelho's *The Alchemist*. We talked about books and music. She loved Jewel and Alanis Morissette. If I played her Stanley Clarke or Steely Dan, she listened appreciatively. Our rapport was good. Until it wasn't.

I was proud to be nominated for an NAACP Image Award as outstanding vocalist. The televised show was in Los Angeles. Given that she was my girlfriend, Emily presumed I would take her. Instead, I invited my mom.

I felt as though Emily resented my decision. She wanted to know whether I had reservations about walking the red carpet with a white woman. That same old subject was back front and center. Part of me probably didn't love the idea of being photographed at such a high-profile event with a white woman. But the bigger issue was that I had never completely committed to Emily. I still didn't view our relationship as permanent. I saw it as a dance that, while delightful at times, could also be awkward, not to mention downright dysfunctional.

Prince, by the way, won the award in my category that night. You can't be mad at losing to a genius. His victory softened the defeat.

The fallout with Emily was severe. For a while she moved to California to study Kabbalah, a form of Jewish mysticism. A restless soul, she relocated to New York. At the same time, our on-and-off relationship was back on.

While it was freezing cold in Detroit, she invited me to Sedona, where her parents lived. They were good people who accepted me without prejudice or judgment. Arizona was fascinating. The dry desert landscape with its mountainous backdrops was something out of a cowboy movie. The sky was enormous, and the red rock formations in Sedona looked like crazy modern sculpture. I dug the huge canyons and the magical sunsets. Away from the tensions of touring, I sat in the middle of a great pine forest on a day trip to Flagstaff. I breathed in the fresh air. Emily took me places I hadn't been before.

During the summer of my fortieth birthday, we drove to Yelton Manor, a beautiful B & B in South Haven on Lake Michigan. For a week, the days were sunny, the nights cool, my head clear. Life was good.

———————

My finances were solid. That's the reason I flew to New York to do something I had longed to do since I started making music: buy a grand piano.

In doing so, I decided not to compromise. I wanted the best. I had first seen the Steinway brand on the piano in my high school music room. When I ran my fingers across those keys, I felt like I was levitating. That thrill never left me. And though I wrote my songs on various electric keyboards—and played those keyboards onstage—I always felt something was missing. A grand acoustic piano was, at least to my ears, the ultimate sound of musical expression. There's nothing wrong with factory-built pianos. But the notion of a hand-crafted piano had a purity and prestige I couldn't resist.

I went to the Steinway showroom in midtown Manhattan, where, under the portraits of virtuosos like Vladimir Horowitz and André Watts, I sat at a dozen pianos until I found the one that spoke to my heart.

Two weeks later, a seven-foot Steinway grand sat in my basement home studio in Lathrup Village. I had arranged for a tuner to come over on the day of its arrival to make the final adjustments. When he left, I touched the keys and silently thanked the divine circumstances that allowed me to possess this magnificent instrument. I knew that my music, in some fundamental way, would change.

I had been using Fender Rhodes sounds to write my songs for years. The Rhodes is cool. The Rhodes provides a built-in warmth. Conversely, for all its grandeur, the Steinway could be cold and temperamental. It left me exposed and vulnerable. I had to provide the warmth. I could manipulate the volume of the Rhodes, but while I could play softer or louder on the Steinway, there were no knobs or buttons that could instantly give me a bigger or a smaller sound.

The Rhodes enveloped my voice in a way that the Steinway did not. Writing on the Steinway meant singing over it, singing out, reaching for melodies with greater height and depth. The Steinway called for a greater vocal architecture: elaborate archways, sweeping angles, vaulted ceilings. It was a challenge I relished.

Suddenly, my work on a suite of new songs for my third album was interrupted by something I had never anticipated:

My father was diagnosed with a deadly cancer.

47

"THE CHILD IS FATHER OF THE MAN"

The English poet William Wordsworth wrote those words over two hundred years ago. Reading them now, they resonate; they have me reflecting on a period of my life when my feelings for my father underwent radical change.

Even when I learned that Erick Hardy was not my biological father, he never stopped being my dad. He was always my old man. I was always his child. But when he got sick, it was as if the child—me—became the father, and the father—Erick Hardy—became the child. The roles reversed. It was frightening and confusing. It came at a time when I was struggling to put together my third album. The emotional fallout was so great that my creative process ground to a halt.

The diagnosis was severe. The cancer was in an advanced stage. I didn't expect Dad to survive. Because colon cancer can be cured if caught early, I wondered whether he had ever undergone a colonoscopy. The answer was no. Dad didn't like doctors and refused to go to them. In some ways, this went against that part of his character—a huge part—that always lectured about responsibility. Men must always do the responsible thing. Yet avoiding self-care was highly irresponsible. I was angry that he had acted so irresponsibly. But I couldn't tell him that, not when he was so sick and so vulnerable.

All of us—his son, his daughters, his wife—went to the hospital for his operation. The tumor was removed, as well as a large portion of his colon. There was also an initial concern that the cancer had spread. The operation was successful, but the aftermath would be hell. The prognosis was dire. When he came home after an extended stay, he was never the same. The particulars of his ongoing maintenance were, for him, both humiliating and agonizing.

I played the part of the dutiful son. I drove him to the treatment center where he sat in a chair and received chemotherapy. Other patients, many of whom looked close to death, were undergoing the same ordeal. I didn't want to be there. I didn't want to hear the insipid Muzak playing over the speakers. I didn't want to see the forlorn look in the eyes of those suffering. But most of all, I didn't want to see my father suffering, fearfully contemplating his mortality.

On the ride home, I wanted to lecture him as he had lectured me earlier in my life. Why hadn't he had regular doctor appointments? Why hadn't he recognized modern medicine's advances and done everything he could to stay healthy?

Beyond chemotherapy, there were radiation treatments. And beyond the treatments themselves, there was severe emotional fallout. His sickness radically altered his relationship with my mother. She, too, was both angry and dutiful. She accepted her new role as caretaker but also resented the imposition of that role. There had always been tension between them. It intensified.

As best we could, we were preparing for what seemed like Dad's inevitable demise. Part of the preparation meant making sure his affairs were in order. They may well have been, but he was the only one who would have known that. We were in the dark about his finances. This angered me at the very moment when compassion required that I not express my fury. The poor man was dying.

In the silence of my mind and in conversations with Mom, I could vent. I could remember the years he spent sitting in his La-Z-Boy chair watching the financial talking heads on CNBC. The years he spent helping me understand that monetary responsibility was all about making the right moves and investing for the future.

But this was not the time to chastise him. I backed off to grant him the same grace I would want to receive if I were in his position. I helped organize the disorder as much as I could, but it was Mom who did the heavy lifting. It took months of hard work.

All this was done intensely because it seemed as though, given Dad's fragile condition, the end was near. That's where the surprise came. He survived. As I write, he's still reclining in the La-Z-Boy and watching *Mad Money* with Jim Cramer on CNBC. There have been many bumps along the way, scary returns to the hospital with life-threatening emergencies. But Erick Hardy, my dad, despite the odds, turned out to be one tough hombre. He'll probably outlive all of us.

Oddly, or maybe inevitably, his challenges brought us closer together. I felt for him. Because he had been so frightened, his obstinacy melted. His self-reliance was diminished. He needed someone to talk to. For the first time in his life, he thanked me for being there. While his health was shattered, his humanity expanded. It was something to witness.

By 2008, he was back on his feet. It was summertime and he felt strong enough to cut the grass. A big deal. While he was outside, the phone rang. It was his sister calling from Florida, where his mother was in hospice at the end of her own battle with cancer. She had only hours left to live and wanted to hear the voice of her firstborn son one last time.

I walked outside and signaled Dad to cut off the mower. He saw the concern in my eyes. I said he'd better come inside. His mother was on the line. I remember silently fussing at God, *Yo! Can't you give this dude a fucking break?*

My mother handed him the phone. He waited several seconds before he said words that I had never heard him say: "I love you, Mama." I stayed close by as he hung up the phone in tears, walked back outside, and finished cutting the lawn.

———————

On September 11, 2007, Maurice Hardy went home to be with the Lord. Four days later my youngest sister, Karmen, would be getting married. Now Dad was obliged to travel to Florida to help his siblings arrange their mother's funeral. Dad couldn't be there to walk his youngest daughter down the aisle as planned, so at the wedding I took his place. Once again, the roles had been reversed.

My father, with whom I had fought bitterly for so many years, needed a son who could act in his place.

48

INTIMACY AND THE FOURTH OF JULY

I faced the phenomenon of fatherhood again in the winter of 2009, when Emily told me she was pregnant.

I received the news with reservations. I wish I could say I was thrilled, but I wasn't. In all ways, I would support Emily and our child, but I knew that Emily and I would never form a family. Yet I wasn't about to shun my responsibility. There were also powerful moments where my discomfort was overshadowed by the radiance of a pregnant Emily. She was aglow.

That image was powerful enough to form a song I began by thinking of my own mother. At the same time, in my mind's eye I was seeing the mother of my unborn child. At the Steinway, I found the right notes to sing over. I found the right message that expressed my heart:

To a mother's love, you are bound
You can rest on a sacred ground
In a mother's love, you are free to dream
Because she sees what you can be . . .

The birth of the song on my third album, *Intimacy*, coincided with the birth of our precious daughter, Laylah, on the Fourth of July in 2010. In the early weeks of her life, she'd look at me with what I thought to be a certain skepticism, as if she knew I hadn't jumped for joy when I learned Emily was carrying her. As the months and years went by, though, joy did enter my heart every time I was with her. Laylah was nothing but joy. She became one of the great blessings of my life.

Other songs from *Intimacy*, especially "Share My Life," expressed my unchangeable desire to do just that — share my life with someone to whom I could finally and unalterably commit. Why wasn't Emily that "someone"? I can't say. I can't find fault with her. I can only say that I undercut a permanent union by succumbing to my old default position: in the face of commitment, I retreated.

I still didn't know how to forge a relationship with a woman.

In short, I was living at a time when my songs said one thing and my life said another. Because songs are written in the moment and capture immediate emotions, I don't question the sincerity of those emotions any more than I question the sincerity of the songs. My emotions were breezes floating on a summer afternoon. They gave relief, they felt wonderful, but they passed.

Because I had two beautiful children, Troi and Laylah, with two beautiful women — Michelle and Emily — and yet remained a single man in search of something I couldn't name, I decided I needed help. I remembered how, after the meltdown I experienced in the wake of the Motown offer, I had benefited from the female perspective of my psychiatrist and decided to go back into therapy.

49

LIGHT SEEKER

Who looks outside, dreams; who looks inside, awakes.

—CARL JUNG

Our initial session consisted of my long-winded attempt to answer the psychiatrist's first question: "What brings you back here?"

The only answer I could give was fear. And to that, the only question she could pose was, "Fear of what?"

I went over all that had happened with Dad. The reality of his mortality had forced me to reflect on mine. Death is always a scary notion, especially when it comes close to taking the most important man in your life. For a long while, she listened as I confessed how his physical deterioration had rocked me to my core.

I confessed something else. In recording *Intimacy*, I had blown out my voice. An ear, nose, and throat doctor had found a small precancerous growth on my left vocal cord. It would require surgery. My mind immediately went to catastrophe. Would this mean I could never sing again? And if so, how would I maintain? I *was* my voice; I *was* my singing, my music, my songs. The only person I'd spoken to about this was my mother, who, as always, was encouraging. But her encouragement didn't lessen my anxiety. I was not comforted after the surgery when I was told all was well. My falsetto, an integral part of my vocal style, was inaccessible. The doctor said I'd improve over time, but I remained anxious.

Hearing all this, the psychiatrist felt we needed to explore my fears even more intensely—which is exactly what I didn't want to do.

That exploration was deep.

The doctor confessed something that surprised me. When I'd first started seeing her, she didn't know my music. Subsequently, she'd begun listening to it. In doing so, she realized that my songs were extremely personal and wondered whether I was willing to use them as a starting point to address some of my issues.

I asked whether she assumed that my songs were, in fact, auto-biographical. She turned the question back on me.

I said some were and some weren't. She accepted my answer while suggesting that several seemed to contain the seeds of my discontent.

I asked for an example.

She mentioned "Love Never Fails." She heard it as a confirmation of the healing power of love. I agreed. She went on to say that she was struck by the word *shame* as it applied to the relationship in the song. I repeat the word no less than three times. The doctor pointed out how I was obsessed with "shame" as I sang the lines, "Have shame on you / And have shame on me."

I asked what she thought it all meant.

She answered by quoting two more lines: "Staying here for so long / When we both know it was so wrong . . ." The doctor went on to explain that love, at least for me, lives in a paradox. It lasts, but it doesn't. It conquers all, except for the shame that surrounds it. She asked whether I could point to a romantic relationship in my adult life that had not carried the weight of shame.

I couldn't. That's when she wondered about my family history. I went into it. The word *shame* had me thinking of my own mother and the fact that I was born into shame. The shame of her seduction by a teacher in her high school. The shame she felt in telling my grandmother that she was pregnant. The shame my grandmother felt when her Pentecostal congregation learned about the scandal. The shame I had felt in all my early sexual encounters.

The doctor listened carefully and confirmed that my history was relevant, but beyond the shame of my distant past, she asked about the source of shame associated with my more recent relationships.

In thinking of Michelle, Sarah, and Emily, I was ashamed of the pain that I had caused them.

My therapist clarified her thoughts in this way:

The end of any relationship is painful. Pain cannot be avoided, but shame is something else entirely. Shame doesn't merely say, "I've done something wrong." Shame says, "I *am* wrong." Shame doesn't say, "I've miscalculated my feelings for this woman." Shame says, "Because I miscalculated my feelings, I have no redeeming value. I'm worthless. I'm bad." Shame makes us turn in on ourselves. Self-anger, self-loathing, self-condemnation—these are the building blocks of depression.

She spoke about how shame exacerbates depression. At the same time, she reminded me feelings of self-worth can assuage depression. Sobriety had led to a series of major positive movements in my life. I was reconciled with my family. I remained present in the lives of my precious daughters, Troi and Laylah. I found God and a faith that sustained me. I was at the point, she stressed, where I was capable of self-acceptance.

But I wondered whether self-acceptance ran the risk of making me complacent. Wouldn't it let me say, "I have things about myself I find hateful, but I'll accept them and go on my merry way"?

The doctor saw it differently. The very fact that I'd come to her told her that I wasn't complacent. By returning to therapy, I was saying the same thing I had said at my first twelve-step meeting. I was saying I needed help. That statement requires humility. And it's only with humility that any of us can face, and try to modify, the negative forces working to bring us down.

———————

I left her office feeling grateful for the conversation. Feeling uplifted. While enlightenment might have been a distant goal, looking for light was something I could do right here and now.

50

HOLDING ON

The *Intimacy* tour was different. I brought the Steinway onstage. I loved the grandeur of it. And I also loved how it helped bring out my voice in a brighter, bolder way. Having written on the Steinway, I saw that my melodies were moving in more of a pop direction. That change seemed natural and right.

While Dave McMurray had left to play with Kid Rock, the presence of my old friend Brian O'Neal filled the void. He had moved back to Detroit and accepted my invitation to join the band. Musically, we had always been soul mates. Brian was one of my first teachers.

When I wasn't seated at the Steinway, I stood center stage at the mic while Brian held down the keys. His accompaniment was far better than my own. His presence freed me up to sing with greater latitude. I also added covers to give the show a lift—Earth, Wind & Fire's "Can't Hide Love," Chaka Khan's "Sweet Thing," the Emotions' "Best of My Love."

I also switched from easy breezy outfits to custom-made suits.
I wanted a more tailored look—fitted jackets, cuff links, pocket
squares, trousers that broke over the top of my blue Ferragamos at
precisely the right point.

Over the course of six weeks, the *Intimacy* tour hit twenty-eight
cities. The response was gratifying. Many of the fans had already
memorized the new songs. Enthusiasm was high. Onstage, I played,
I sang, I testified, I stayed in the moment. But once the shows were
over, I felt down. Call it melancholy. Call it free-floating anxiety.
I wasn't sure what to call it. I wasn't sure what was going on in my
heart and in my head. All I knew was that I felt unsettled.

One night after I played a show in Los Angeles, I couldn't sleep. My
Beverly Hills hotel room felt stultifying. I decided to get out and go
for a drive. I threw on a tracksuit and called for my car. The city was
fast asleep. I followed Wilshire Boulevard all the way west to Santa
Monica and then Highway 1 up the coast to Malibu. I rolled down
the windows to breathe in the cool night air. The ocean had a salty
fragrance that refreshed my spirit. I stopped when I reached the Malibu pier. Aside from a few people dangling their fishing poles into
the water, it was deserted. The Pacific was calm. Moonlight gave the
ocean a silvery gleam. Seagulls fluttered above. Stars crowded the
sky. Tears came to my eyes. I wasn't sure why.

Standing at the very end of the pier, staring out into infinite
space, I tried to look into my soul, into a darkness of twisted and
tangled emotions. What created this darkness? I still felt guilty about
being unfaithful to Sarah. I was ashamed that I had undercut my
relationship with Emily. I was not able to be a live-in dad for either
of my daughters. A voice said things had been going too well, disas-

ter was heading my way. I started catastrophizing about my future. I imagined that, after this tour, I would not be able to sing again. I had no evidence of that, but I didn't need evidence. Because I had been careless with the lives of others, I should not expect that good things would continue happening for me.

I would surely reap what had been sown. Calamity was incoming.

And yet . . . The moonlight on the water, the starlit sky, and the soft breeze were working to ease me from my panicked state. I thought of the fundamentals of my faith. Of all the twelve steps, I turned to the one that resonated most deeply, the eleventh: "Sought through prayer and meditation to improve our conscious contact with God as we understood Him, praying only for knowledge of His will for us and the power to carry that out." Looking out at the ocean, I reminded myself that if the eleventh step was right, I didn't have to pray for my voice to be forever strong or even for my guilt and shame to be lifted. I didn't have to solicit God for any single worldly thing. My prayer was for knowledge of his will, a direction generated by spirit. I'd have to surrender and submit to that spirit.

My chain of thought was interrupted by the sight of one of the fishermen reeling in a catch. When he saw that the fish wasn't big enough, he threw it back into the deep. A patient man, he began the process all over again. While observing the fisherman, I plunged deeper into thought. How do you know when you're being willful as opposed to willing? My ego may be saying that God's will is that I remain healthy through old age. I want that ego to be right. I don't hate my ego. Nor can I lose my ego. Ego serves a purpose. Gives us drive. Helps us achieve. But I remembered my recovery friend saying how overblown, self-obsessed ego could destroy me. Standing at the end of the pier, I knew that was true. I couldn't bend God's will to mine. I had to bend my will to his. Which means making room for the idea that no matter which way my life goes, I can let go of the results, trusting that God is going to move through me to facilitate what he wants. I don't have to know what that is. I just have to trust in his goodness. I just have to keep turning my life over, day after day after day.

It all came down to a cliché I'd heard all too often in recovery circles: *Easy does it*. I was alone but I was not alone. I did not have to seek God's love. I simply had to receive it. Embrace it. And keep moving forward.

I couldn't put my finger on it, but innately I knew something was missing. It wasn't musical success. I had that. It wasn't family. Things were finally good in that department. I had my faith and sobriety, yet my soul was restless.

When I reached the hotel and climbed back into the bed, I opened the curtains. The night was receding. The sky was a bluish gray. The light gave me hope. But I knew that the season of my discontent wasn't completely over. The struggle for spiritual clarity would continue. And, true to form, I turned my struggle into song. I picked up a yellow pad and started to write . . .

The will to love means
Keeping still, my love,
Knowing love will surely arrive
At a time unknown
In a place unseen

Sleep came easily but I woke up feeling alone.

———

In the months that followed, romance continued to elude me. One woman, a dancer I met on a cruise, was especially sensuous. Another, a hostess at a restaurant, was especially beautiful. Yet neither relationship, though each was sexually exciting, lasted long. The spiritual connection wasn't there. I mainly kept to myself. When I traveled, I traveled alone. I had no entourage, no posse, no one scouting the audience for potential hookups on my behalf. In a way, my acute shyness protected me from taking even deeper dives into sexual dysfunction.

Soon I would be back home in Detroit, back at the Steinway, plucking my way into another groove—searching for the lost chord.

51

PROMISE TO LOVE

In 2013, at age forty-six, I wrote the title song of what would become my new album, *Promise to Love*. The lyrics were about cherishing a woman. I sang to a woman whom I did not know, admitting that I had crazily been running around while she waited patiently. I knew her love was sacred, and I vowed to cherish her for the rest of my life. I asked the Lord to shine his light on our love.

After the release of the title track, many people told me that they'd played "Promise to Love" at their nuptials. Without realizing it, I had written a wedding song, although at the time I had no romantic attachment. Marriage was the last thing on my mind.

I included on the album a song that said, "Pray for me." It was a meditation on my spiritual path. "If we walk by what we see," I wrote, "then we may never ever be free." I was praying for more faith. "A little more faith," I sang, "is all I need."

In short, the album opens with a promise and ends with a prayer.

But what was I promising and to whom was I praying? The songs were born not out of my head but out of my heart. And my heart was imagining something that my head could not yet see.

———————

November 2015. The Fox Theatre. Atlanta.

My *Promise to Love* tour was the first to include two female dancers, who enhanced our show with their grace and flair. I also paid more attention to lighting and background graphics. I remembered how Luther Vandross, during his fabled concerts, lavishly costumed his dancers and singers. He realized it was the star's obligation to turn a show into an event. He liked telling his audience, "I don't play with your ticket money." He knew that, for their hard-earned money, they deserved all he could give. I tried to follow Luther's lead.

My management team, along with the promoter, had set up two VIP packages for those who wanted to meet me before the show. The first was for a group of twenty or so people. They came backstage, and after a brief chat, pictures were taken. The second group was smaller and eager for a deeper, more personal experience. There were only three people—a married couple and an attractive woman who introduced herself as Erica. The couple asked several questions about my approach to songwriting. Through articles they had read, they knew something of my story and were also curious about my spiritual life. I appreciated their interest. Our conversation was deep. Meanwhile, Erica, whose eyes were bright and smile even brighter, said little. Yet her spirit said a great deal. I could feel her energy. She sparkled. Though she asked me no questions, she brought two vinyls—the kind used by deejays—and asked me to sign them. I asked her if she was, in fact, a deejay.

"It's something I'm transitioning into," she said.

"Do you have a card?" I asked.

"I don't."

I immediately felt stupid. "Do you have a card?" What a lame-ass question. Who carries business cards in this day and age? I had only asked for a card because I wanted to holler at her without everyone in the room knowing I was hollering at her.

Before every show, I have a prayer circle for the musicians and crew who wish to participate. Erica's spirit prompted me to ask her to join. She readily accepted. She stood next to me. I took her hand. We both bowed our heads as I said, "Father God, we acknowledge your loving presence. We thank you for our gifts and ask that our work be received in the name of love."

I noticed that during my first song she stayed in the wings before moving to her seat in the front row. I had this feeling that, without consciously trying, I was singing to her. This had never happened before. It was never my style to sing to an individual woman in the audience. When the show was over, I looked at her and gave her a little wave. She smiled and waved back.

Something told me that I was at the beginning of a story.

After our first encounter, I reached out to her on Instagram to make known my intent to keep in touch. I tried to disguise that intent by asking her what she thought of the show. Maybe it was a silly question. But I guess I was also looking for some reassurance. She offered me just that. She said she loved it. The word *love* struck my heart. We continued writing one another little messages.

They were simple and short.

She asked whether I still lived in Detroit. Yes.

I asked about her home. A small city twenty miles south of Atlanta. Was that where she grew up? It was.

I wondered about her work. Deejaying turned out to be a sideline. Her main job was with a freight-forwarding firm. The pay was good. Her computer skills were superb. She was highly accomplished at resolving logistical problems.

The messages made me comfortable and uncomfortable at the same time. I'm not much of a chitchatter, and I didn't want to come on too strong. I was comforted by the fact that Erica wanted to keep in touch as much as I did. I was uncomfortable asking questions that may have been too personal. I kept it light, knowing all the time that my feelings were anything but.

I had dreams, and later I learned Erica had had dreams as well. The dreams weren't sexual. They were abstract. I saw Erica in some divine light. The first song of *Promise to Love* is "Saving My Love for You." It says, "Ever since time was young, / Ever since there were trees and sun, / Long before earth was new, / I've been saving my love for you." I sang, "Long before land and sea, / Long before life had come to be, / Even all the angels knew, / I'd be saving my love for you."

The images from the song—mountains and streams, rainbows and marigolds—populated my dreams. I saw Erica seated at the center of a luminous rainbow. I saw Erica walking through a field of golden marigolds. I saw Erica bathing beneath a tropical waterfall. I saw her in a lush forest, on a misty mountain. In one dream she was flying through a cloudless sky. I tried to catch her, but I couldn't sprout wings, and seeing I was losing her as she sailed into the crimson sunset, I woke up in a cold sweat. I was afraid I had lost her. Yeah, I had it bad.

Of course, I didn't share any of this with Erica. I could have said, "We can move mountains and dance among the stars," but it probably would have scared her to death. My feelings were based on . . . what? One twenty-minute backstage meeting and a few Instagram messages. My hunger for a real relationship might well have been clouding my mind and defining my dreams. And yet, if I was pressed, I'd have to say that I felt pushed by something that had more than a hint of divinity. I was moving into new territory. Part of me was anxious. The prospect of deceiving myself was frightening. I didn't want to be disappointed, nor did I want to disappoint her. But another part of me was more excited than I wanted to admit.

52

LET'S GET PERSONAL

My personal life was busy. Beyond touring, I did my best to spend as much time with Troi and Laylah as possible. That wasn't always easy because they also kept busy schedules. But I loved my girls and understood how vital it was for the father-daughter bond to stay strong.

Erica stayed on my mind. Our relationship, though, was still restricted to emails and texts. Little by little, the messages got deeper. She asked if I was happy. I didn't have a ready answer so I asked her the same question. Her reply revealed one of her strongest traits: She said that she tried to stay positive. She sought to see the bright side of things and the best in people. I liked hearing that.

Enough texting. It was time to call. I worked up the nerve to make the first call as Christmas was approaching.

During our first conversation, things got personal in a hurry. She asked me if I was "reserved." I answered that I was. A long silence.

What was wrong? By "reserved," I thought she was asking if I was shy. I was—and am—certainly shy. But instead, she simply wanted to know if I was attached to another woman. It took us a minute to clear things up, but I assured her that I was not in a relationship.

I was smiling and guessed that she was too.

We began exchanging information about our pasts. No, I had never been married, but yes, I had two daughters, Troi, twenty, and Laylah, five, who lived with their moms. I added that both my children were biracial. That's when she told me that she also had a biracial daughter, Alex, who was seven.

It felt good to know that we had something extremely significant in common. She spoke lovingly about Alex and called her the main focus of her life. She also said that she had not married John, Alex's dad.

We got into the subject of earlier romantic experiences. She told me she'd had a white boyfriend in high school.

In turn, I spoke about my past relationships with white women.

We realized that prejudice wasn't an issue for either of us. We were comforted to have this history in common and open enough to discuss it without judgment.

The deeper our conversation got, the more the telephone seemed an inadequate way to exchange all our ideas and feelings. That's when I heard myself saying something I hadn't expected to say.

"I'd like to see you."

My statement hung out there for several long seconds until Erica replied.

"Well, I'd like to see you too."

More silent awkwardness.

From there, it was a matter of logistics. Would she like to come to Detroit or prefer that I fly down to Atlanta? She was happy either way. Because I tend to be deliberative, I asked if she'd mind if I gave it some thought. She told me to take all the time I needed.

For all her perkiness and high spirits, Erica was very laid-back. I liked that about her. I liked so many things about her. In my own laid-back way, I was as excited as she was about the prospect of meeting up again.

If she came to Detroit, would it be presumptuous to ask her to stay with me? Probably so. Which is why I decided to fly to Atlanta. We would usher in 2016 together.

53

A REASON TO REJOICE

I was more worked up than I wanted to admit. I wanted to keep a cool veneer, but how cool could I be? I couldn't get my mind off this beguiling woman. I booked a suite at the Ritz-Carlton and arranged for her to be picked up from home, some twenty miles outside Atlanta. Was that cool? Should I have rented a car and picked her up myself? I wasn't sure. I wanted to be a gentleman. I *was* a gentleman, so why was I trying to prove it? Was I overdoing it? I was so eager to see this woman—whom I had only seen once before but who had been dancing around in my dreams—that I stood in front of the hotel for thirty minutes before she was due to arrive. When I saw a pristine black SUV pull up, I was right there to open the door, only to see an elderly Asian couple emerge. They thought I was the valet. Didn't matter. I smiled and wished them a good evening. But where was Erica? Seemed like every vehicle pulling up was a chauffeured Cadillac Escalade or Lincoln Navigator. Another one dropped off a businessman as wide as he was tall. A third deposited a group of elderly ladies dressed in white gloves and fancy hats. Could my driver have gotten lost? Could Erica have changed her mind?

Finally, I did what I should have done in the first place—I called Erica and tried not to sound too anxious. She assured me that she'd be pulling up in five minutes.

When her car did arrive, I let the driver get the door. Her smile was even brighter than I'd remembered. My heart started racing. I reached out my hand to help her out of the car. Her hand was warm. I wanted to hug her but—*Keep your cool, Kim*—kissed her on the cheek instead. Her skin was soft.

I asked if she was hungry. She was. How about sushi? Sushi would be great.

When we started walking, I took Erica's hand.

"You don't have to do that," she said.

"What do you mean?" I asked.

"You don't have to hold my hand. I mean, this isn't really a date, is it?"

"Girl, I just flew from Detroit to Atlanta to take you out on New Year's Eve. This is definitely a date!"

The sushi restaurant was decorated in light wood. The walls were covered with color photographs of Japanese silk fans and vintage kimonos. We sat at a secluded corner table. A small candle gave off the fragrance of lilac. Flickers of light illuminated Erica's face so that her eyes, mouth, and lips appeared even more enchanting. Not that I needed more enchantment. I had been enchanted the first day we met.

It was hard not to be impressed when, in her modest way, Erica talked about owning her own house, holding down this solid job, raising her daughter as a single mom, and, on top of all that, being enrolled at Clayton State University.

In between bites of our California rolls, talk came easily. Our rapport felt natural. Erica was gregarious. Her bubbly personality counteracted my introverted and guarded nature.

I let Erica know we had a big decision to make. After dinner, we could go to either a comedy club or church.

She laughed and quickly chose church. She described herself as being brought up in the church. Church, she said, was always good for the soul. Even on New Year's Eve? I wondered. Especially on New Year's Eve, she assured me.

I explained that my lawyer, Denise Brown, was not only a brilliant Black woman but an inspiring preacher studying for a PhD. Erica had heard of Denise's church, Christians for Change, because a friend of hers played in the church band.

All good. I was with a woman who was not only willing but eager to go to church on New Year's Eve. I couldn't have been happier. We toasted each other with glasses of sparkling water, nibbled on our sushi, and spoke about our daughters. I called for the car, and during the twenty-five-minute drive to Denise's church, we stayed mainly silent, our hands intertwined.

The church was small, spirit filled, and well attended.

Denise didn't preach that night but did sit beside us. She had been flawlessly supervising my legal matters for years. But unlike many overly aggressive lawyers, Denise had a firm yet gentle touch. Without ignoring her practice, she pursued a scholarly study of the Bible and fulfilled her calling to preach. Lawyer Denise and Minister Denise were one and the same. Each strove to communicate on a loving level. After the services, she spoke to us outside the church.

"There is reason to rejoice tonight," said Denise. "The start of a new year is always exciting because it reinforces the possibility of positive change. But, Kem and Erica, there's another reason I'm feeling so happy . . ." At this moment, her eyes filled with tears. Softly, Denise began crying. She regained her composure and said, "I can see the love that you have for one another. And that love feels divine."

Erica was tearing up as well. I did all I could not to start crying myself. When Denise left, Erica said, "I hope we'll see her again soon."

"We will," I promised.

54

"SO BEAUTIFUL"

On the ride back to the hotel, Erica mentioned that Denise had a beautiful soul. I nodded. We were silent for the rest of the trip. Wondering if Erica wanted to be driven home, I broke the silence by asking if she'd rather go home or to the hotel. She preferred the hotel.

The suite was on the lavish side. There was a large living room with a slate-gray velvet couch facing two matching lounge chairs and a wide-screen television. Erica sat on the couch. I sat in one of the easy chairs.

She told me how she had almost come to see me perform at an earlier Atlanta show I had done with Charlie Wilson. I wondered what had stopped her. She said the VIP ticket was expensive, and at the time she was hesitant to spend that kind of money. I wanted to know why it was so important to have a VIP ticket. She hesitated before explaining that she felt compelled to meet me—and a VIP ticket was the only way. Why, I wondered, did she feel compelled?

That's when she mentioned dreams. She described herself, in the least pretentious way, as something of a seer. She'd had dreams about meeting me and felt to not do so would dishonor a vision that had appeared over and over again.

I was taken aback. I didn't doubt it, but it was a heavy thing to hear. I lightened things up by asking about her hobbies. She mentioned motorcycles. I was surprised to learn that five years ago, after taking a Harley-Davidson class, she'd bought a bike, a Suzuki GSX-R600.

"So you had the helmet, the leather jacket, the gloves . . . the whole bit?" I asked.

"I did," Erica confirmed.

I sat and looked at this woman. Beyond her smile—though it was hard to get beyond her smile—there was something so sincere and sweet about her that I started asking myself: *Is she too good to be true?*

Our conversation got deeper. I jokingly asked whether this Suzuki indicated a wild side to her character. She didn't want to call it wild, though she did say there had been a period when she socialized too much.

I relaxed a bit, but I wondered what she meant by "socialized too much."

"I was trying to cope with the death of my dad and my maternal grandmother. They passed within two weeks of each other. Emotionally, I didn't know how to deal with grief."

In this same period, the man with whom she was romantically involved had left their relationship. That also hurt.

My curiosity was piqued. I wanted to ask many more questions. I wanted to know more about Erica. I wanted to know everything about Erica. What about the father of her daughter, John? How had that relationship started and stopped? But I turned off my mind and went to my heart. My heart said, *Give this woman room to breathe. Don't give her the third degree. Ask her if she'd like to watch a movie.*

"Sure thing," said Erica.

"You choose," I said, handing her the remote.

She chose *The Martian*. I was hoping she might pick something more romantic, but I was happy to see her excited by the prospect of our watching a movie together. I moved over and sat next to her on the couch. We held hands.

The story takes place twenty years in the future. Matt Damon is Mark Watney, a botanist on a scientific mission to Mars. Through extraordinary circumstances, he finds himself alone on the planet, where he must rely on his remarkable intellectual resources—as well as his grit—to survive. The theme of survival resonated with us both. We were pulling for Watney to make it, and when he did, we applauded his feat. I was grateful for the upbeat story. The vibe between us was more positive than ever. It was two a.m., and neither of us wanted the night to end.

Musiq Soulchild's "So Beautiful" played softly in the background. The haunting ballad said exactly what I wanted to say. A man wants to give a woman all his love, not just for a night but for the rest of his life. He wants to be by her side forever. "So Beautiful" became our song. I remember thinking, though I kept myself from saying it, that I loved this woman. I didn't say it because this was our first date. I also didn't say it because I didn't totally trust my emotions. I didn't totally trust my timing. But the truth is that my heart was happier than it had been in years.

It felt right to kiss Erica, and when I did, she didn't resist. The kiss was meaningful. Looking back, I can also say that the kiss was life changing.

Strange as it might seem, both of us realized that this was neither the time nor the place to sexually consummate our feelings.

It was way too soon. I recognized, just as she recognized, the need for patience. We understood that something potentially serious was happening. That "something" required time to unfold.

Erica fell asleep on the couch. I covered her with a blanket. I took the other end of the couch and drifted off. I can't remember my dreams, but I can recall the feeling of floating. I was sleeping on a cloud. At daybreak, we opened our eyes at the same time. There was that smile of hers.

I ordered breakfast from room service.

Fresh orange juice and toast with jam. Crisp bacon. Two café lattes. We chatted about this and that. All light, all easy. Our unspoken communication was even stronger than the verbal vibe.

I kissed her on the cheek and asked her if she'd like me to ride with her when the car drove her home.

"It's fine," she said. "I know you have things to do."

We hugged, held hands in the elevator, held hands walking across the lobby, and waited for our driver to pull up. Another kiss. A long hug. I put my hand on her cheek, felt the softness of her skin, felt a giddiness in my spirit, felt like a million bucks.

Moments after she was whisked away in the shiny black Escalade, I realized that I was already missing her.

55

JOY AND PAIN

Erica and I were feeling the groove like every other fan rocking out at the Frankie Beverly and Maze concert in San Diego. Maze concerts are like Black family reunions where everyone is invited to join the love-in. Frankie played "Southern Girl"—and of course I thought of Erica. He sang "Back in Stride," "Golden Time of Day," "Happy Feelings." But it was "Joy and Pain" that hit me hardest. It's about the beauty of falling in love, the heady combination of sunshine and rain that lightens and darkens our lives.

After the show, I took Erica backstage to meet Frankie, whom I knew from doing shows together over the years. Goodwill all around. Erica and I decided to drive over to Coronado Island for a late dinner at an Italian restaurant facing the harbor and glittering skyscrapers of downtown San Diego. The city lights, no matter how glamorous, didn't distract me from the light in Erica's eyes.

Her eyes were smiling. Later we strolled along a pathway at the water's edge. The night was balmy, the sky clear, the stars ablaze.

We started talking about joy and pain. She wanted to hear more about my life before sobriety. I opened up, and the story spilled out. I wanted to hear about her life before the birth of her daughter, Alex. There had been joy—a loving grandmother, the family matriarch, whose last name was Hand. I thought of Bill Withers's song "Grandma's Hands" and said, "So you really had a Grandma Hand." "A God-loving Grandma Hand," she replied. Her sister, Carla, was eight years Erica's senior. Her mother had majored in accounting in college and worked in retail and real estate. The pain came when Erica was two and her father, diagnosed with schizophrenia, suffered a complete breakdown. The circumstances were mysterious, but the aftermath was clear: Erica's parents got divorced and her father moved out. He did recover and had become a designer of computer software. Erica had maintained a relationship with him until his death in 2013. She described him as a brilliant but shy man who protected his privacy and spent endless hours in his basement toying with his computers. She called him a "solitary soul." I wondered if I also fit that description.

In time, Erica's mother would go on to marry an electrical engineer, a military man big on discipline. During those early years, she endured ongoing sexual abuse by both male and female kids. She told no one. She absorbed the shame and somehow carried on. Sexual stimulation, coming at an age when she had no way to grasp its impact, frightened and confused her.

I was amazed that, having gone through such harrowing experiences, she had emerged with such an ebullient personality. Was her natural happiness powerful enough to minimize the effects of abuse?

When we reached a bench, we paused to sit. The rippling water reflected the luminous moon. I thought of the rippling effect of the abuse that I had experienced. I shared those stories with Erica. There were tears in her eyes, tears in mine, the ripples and the tears, the fears from the past, surfacing in the present. That evening we slept separately. In the morning Erica said that her dreams had been dark. I said that mine might have been darker. We rode to the airport, our fingers interlocked, feeling close and sad that we were flying off in different directions.

I closed my eyes as the plane reached cruising altitude, dreaming of the day when I could see Erica again.

56

THE STRENGTH OF SPIRIT

In February of 2016 Erica came to Detroit for Valentine's Day. It was her first visit to the city. We'd been seeing each other for nearly two months. The relationship remained platonic. That was a mutual decision. It wasn't easy but it was right. Love felt like a certainty, but there still was so much to learn about each other. We were hurrying up while taking our time.

Driving to the airport, eager to see Erica again—eager to show her my city and my house, eager for her to meet my mom—I flipped on the radio and, by chance, heard my song "Saving My Love for You."

Again, I wondered whether I'd written the song for the woman I was about to pick up at the airport even before I knew she existed. I was certain I had. Listening to the lyrics, I realized I was talking about a divine love living outside the bounds of our linear lives.

Erica was thrilled to be on my home turf. She understood the depths of my emotional link to the city. She wanted to see it all. For-tunately, she arrived at a moment when long-suffering Detroit was experiencing a renaissance. There had been attempts to rebuild the core of the city before, but this felt like a different season. Of course, Erica arrived with her own brand of optimism. Her spirit was irre-pressible. Just as she saw the good in everyone, she sought to see the beauty of Detroit, the elegant downtown skyscrapers from an earlier era, the urban gardens planted where inner-city houses had been demolished, the midtown Charles H. Wright Museum of African American History, whose permanent exhibition *And Still We Rise* documents the indomitable courage of Black Americans.

The night before Valentine's Day we dined at the Selden Stan-dard in Cass Corridor, a cool restaurant in a gentrified section of the city. Good food, good vibes. It seemed like the right place to disclose more of my past, since so much of my past had happened within miles of where we were seated. I allowed myself to be more vulnerable in Erica's presence. She returned the favor by discussing more of her early life.

Despite the sexual trauma, her childhood and teen years had not been without joy. She had played the flute since fifth grade. She loved being in the marching band. Though she was too modest to brag, she displayed superb musicianship. She told me an endear-ing story about how her high school band teacher, a white trumpet player named Mr. Ryan, would single her out to play a solo in front of the others. She hated that.

Erica loved being a part of things but not the center of attention. She also feared making mistakes in public. She was uncomfortable being out front. It was Mr. Ryan who helped break down her reluc-tance to shine.

Before that, she had played the flute for her grandparents' fifti-eth anniversary. After her rendition of "Swing Low, Sweet Chariot," her entire family applauded while Erica ran into the next room and cried. I asked why.

"I had hit a wrong note," she said.

I could relate. Perfectionism is a harsh taskmaster.

I wasn't surprised that she had graduated in the top 10 percent of her class. Her drive to succeed was a powerful part of her personality.

Sitting across the table from her, I realized we hadn't had a single argument. Not a single disagreement. The exchange of information continued.

Her high school sweetheart was named Michael. He was white. I asked whether his whiteness made him more attractive. She said it wasn't the color of his skin that attracted her as much as his personality. He wasn't pushy. He was passive. After what she'd been through, she couldn't have an aggressive boyfriend. They had music in common. He played tuba. They'd met in middle school. Michael made her comfortable. They went together for four years. He gave her a promise ring. Michael never complained that she always wore baggy clothes. He understood that she didn't want to expose her figure in any obvious way.

She still carried the trauma of what had happened to her as a young girl. The dark images of the abuse she experienced and the feelings of shame that accompanied them were unrelenting. But Michael was gentle, and their physical relationship was good. He had a calming effect on her. He helped her get through her teen years.

I asked how and why it had ended.

For all his gentleness, Michael may not have been faithful. In describing this, though, Erica didn't sound bitter. Bitterness was not part of her character.

She was far more complex than I realized. At this same dinner at the Selden Standard, she candidly spoke about her rebellious days.

There had been times she rode her Suzuki when she was high. I asked her what had brought her out of that darkness.

"I looked at the choice in front of me," she said. "I could spiral out or I could settle down. There was a crazy side to me and a sane side. The crazy side wanted to get crazier, but the sane side said, 'You have a daughter. You have a job. You have a house. You have God. Put the craziness down and stop playing with fire.' So I stopped the partying and drinking. I stopped cold."

I had to say that I could never do that. I needed a program. She understood that my program became my path. We all have different paths. She mentioned again that sometimes she saw her path—and the paths of others—in dreams. That's when she mentioned her cousin Juaquim.

Four years ago, Erica had been riding her Suzuki when she saw her cousin on his crotch-rocket bike. They'd been out of touch and quickly reconnected. They learned that they had this cycling world in common. Erica invited Juaquim to her twenty-fifth birthday party. He arrived on his custom chopper. Her family was glad to see him. But Erica sensed something was wrong. He seemed different. There was a dark aura surrounding him. A few nights later she dreamed about him. She envisioned symbols suggesting impending doom. She woke up frightened.

Three days later she was driving to work. Traffic was worse than usual. When she got to her job, a coworker said there had been a fatal accident at a certain juncture. Erica realized she had passed by that very juncture. Then a family member called to say that it was Juaquim. He had been riding his bike when an eighteen-wheeler struck him and dragged him down the highway for a mile. His death, which she had sensed in the dream, devastated Erica.

In her dreams, she had also seen our future.

"If I hadn't," she said, "I would never have bought the VIP ticket.

I called three friends who I hoped would tell me I was insane for buying the ticket. These were friends who know me well. One was actually Devon, the drummer at the Christians for Change church. I was astonished when all three said the same thing: 'Go!' 'Based on what? Based on my dreams?' I asked them. 'Trust your dreams,' they said. 'Follow your dreams.' And, well, here I am."

I took her hand and brought it to my lips.

57

POSSIBILITY

We had Valentine's dinner at Coach Insignia, the revolving restaurant atop the seventy-three-story Renaissance Center, the iconic Detroit skyscraper that now serves as General Motors' world headquarters. The RenCen, built in 1977, still stands as the city's most prominent monument to high expectations. From the Ambassador Bridge to the skyline of downtown Detroit, the views are spectacular. We were sitting in the clouds. We were on top of the world watching the sun melt into the Detroit River. I had given Erica two dozen red roses. I had ordered the most expensive mineral water money could buy. Fresh lobster. Black-truffle French fries. Lemon vanilla rose cake. Dragon pearl jasmine tea.

We talked about music. About how she discovered that her biological father had himself been a deejay when he gave his equipment to one of Erica's cousins. She didn't resent that because she and her dad had never discussed his interest in music. Silence, which had hung over so much of my life, had also hung over hers. Once again, silence became the subject. She talked about the long silence that surrounded her abuse, which was only broken when, in 2011, a close friend of the family announced that she, too, had been molested. In fact, she had been molested by one of the same people who abused Erica. When this revelation was met with doubt, Erica backed her up. For the first time, she told her family what had happened to her. And for the first time, to deal with the unspoken pain and shame, she went into therapy.

Therapy helped break the shackles of silence, and music, always a source of comfort for her, was also a source of healing. Erica spoke of her love for Michael Jackson's music. We were both crazy for Sade; Anita Baker; Grover Washington Jr.; Earth, Wind & Fire; Smokey Robinson; Luther; Prince; and the SOS Band. Erica told me how every night without fail she listened to the quiet-storm version of the Art of Noise's "Moments in Love."

"I lived inside that song," she said. "I felt like songs spoke to me directly. Does that make sense?"

It did. It made perfect sense.

For all our talk over the past weeks, we'd never discussed Erica's relationship with John, the father of her daughter, Alex. Strange that the topic should come up on Valentine's Day. Erica had spoken with Alex that morning, who'd mentioned that her dad had called her to express his love. Erica did all she could to encourage a strong father-daughter rapport. She discussed meeting John, who was ten years older than her, in 2004, the year she graduated high school. Erica was seventeen. I wondered why, given her high grades, she didn't go straight to college.

"My parents weren't all that supportive of that," she said. "Because I didn't have a clear idea of my occupational goals—I couldn't say that I wanted to be a lawyer or doctor—the feeling in our household was that you go straight to work and start earning. I had good computer skills and a head for business. It wasn't difficult finding work at the freight-forwarding firm."

That's where Erica met John, a customer of the company that had hired her.

"I'd characterize my relationship with John as more dysfunctional than romantic. When we lived together, he could be a bit melancholy," she said. "I thought my job was to lift him up, give him hope, keep his spirit strong. Big mistake. Our relationship ended when Alex was six months old. I was thrilled to have a baby. My intention was to co-parent, but circumstances changed and I became the primary parent. To save money, I moved in with my mother. That didn't work out, which is how I decided to buy my first home during the 2009 recession. I was cool living alone with Alex. She changed my life and deepened my notion of love."

As Erica said the words *notion of love*, I felt my head spinning just as the revolving restaurant had been slowly spinning, giving me a 360-degree view of what appeared to be Detroit's past, present, and future. Detroit contained my past even as it contained my present. But I knew, enchanted by Erica and the openness with which she spoke about herself and her daughter, that my future was with her. No other path seemed possible.

58

THE BOUNDARIES OF LOVE

Late at night, unable to sleep, I wrote these words:

Friends and fathers
Mothers and sons
We're bound together
To love as one

But tensions arise
And threaten and strain
Exploding like storms
Of tropical rain

Will love be drowned?
Will bonds be broken?

Will fellowships die
Over words unspoken?

The boundaries of love
Lord, make them clear
Don't let them turn
To pain and fear

As I was falling in love with Erica, I thought about this idea of boundaries. We had established boundaries that worked well. We had postponed sex so that, first and foremost, we could become friends. We enjoyed one another's company. When she spoke, I didn't interrupt her, and she always gave me room to say whatever was on my mind. She laughed at my lame jokes. She was sensitive to my feelings and vice versa. She put up with my moods, and, because her mood was always so positive, I never had to cheer her up. Erica emanated enough good cheer for the both of us. The result was a profound relaxation I had never felt before with a woman. We were building this foundation of friendship, based on not whimsical infatuation or supercharged lust but emotional reality. Two complex human beings connected by a currency that felt divine.

Erica had not dealt with the challenges of her life perfectly. Neither had I. None of us do. But she had faced those challenges with integrity and courage. She had been able to create healthy boundaries with the important people in her life. I had tried to do the same. Little did I know that I'd face an especially tough challenge in that very area in my own life.

———

One of my more important relationships was with Brian O'Neal, whom I'd known since high school. Musically, Brian was always far more advanced than I was. I wrote my first songs with Brian. When he joined my band, I was elated. I was also elated after we played a benefit for NBA star Dikembe Mutombo's charitable foundation. It happened at the St. Regis hotel in Atlanta, where I was backed by a quartet with Brian on keys. I thought we'd performed well. You can imagine my surprise, then, when after the gig a band member said Brian had expressed some harsh feelings he had for me. He was completely beside himself with frustration, and I didn't understand why.

We were outside the hotel—I was with Erica—and were about to get in our car. Brian was smoking one of his signature Marlboro Lights.

"I heard you were unhappy about the show," I said. "What part of the show?"

"The part where you do your God thing. It's always been hard for me to hear it, but tonight it was like I was being slapped in the face. I almost got up and walked off the stage."

I was stunned. It wasn't that this was the first time I'd been criticized for talking about my faith during my shows. Some church folk felt it belonged in church. And some secular folk felt they just came for music and weren't interested in spiritual talk. Yet for me it was the very reason I was performing. Without my faith walk, I'd never be onstage. There would be no show. My position was clear: Next to my faith, music is secondary. Faith was the foundation of everything. And it didn't matter if anyone found it offensive. I felt it necessary to let my listeners know that the hand of God had been on my life. Not only that, but I also wanted them to know that same grace, mercy, and love were available to them too. I wasn't conducting a praise and worship ceremony. But I was witnessing. The fact that Brian found it repulsive didn't exactly come as a surprise. I had heard those rumblings and felt his eyes rolling every time I did my "God thing." But this was the first time he had spoken about it openly and with such vitriol.

I didn't say anything until the next day, when I'd flown back to Detroit. I texted Brian to say, "Let's talk."

"Okay. Next time you're in Detroit."

"I'm in Detroit now. Let's talk tonight."

"Nah, I can't tonight."

"When would be the best time for you?"

"Not sure."

The texts stopped there. Now I was pissed. I thought to myself: *If this is such a burning issue that Brian was about to storm off the stage, what's keeping him from talking about it? Why can't he make time to discuss it in person? Obviously, it's been bugging him for years. Why can't we get into it and vent our feelings?*

We were only a week away from a gig the following weekend. That made it more imperative to talk to Brian. I told Erica what had happened and that I was really struggling with when would be the best time to call him. Erica asked, "Call him for what?" She was right. His silence said it all. I took him out of the lineup, thinking it would force him to reach out to me. But he didn't reach out. He didn't call. Didn't text. As far as I was concerned, he'd quit.

I felt pressed to establish a boundary. I could no longer keep doing what I did with the knowledge that someone as close and important to me as Brian was so put off by my public stance. Of course, he had a right to his feelings. And while I do believe in witnessing, I'm not a proselytizer. I'd never insist that people believe what I believe. But a band is a close-knit family unit. And to have one of the founding family members tell me that an essential segment of my show was repugnant, well, that crossed a boundary. I couldn't ignore his disapproval. Replacing him wouldn't be easy. In fact, it required hiring two fine musicians to take his place. I missed Brian's presence and his artistry. Yet I knew myself well enough to recognize a simple fact: Onstage, as I spoke of the power of love to transform lives, I needed to feel the support of those closest to me. I needed to feel that they had my back.

59

PROPHECY AND FULFILLMENT

What I needed most was Erica.

It was early 2016 when she came to Detroit for another visit. I was so eager to see Erica, I arrived at the airport an hour early. When she came down the escalator, she was glowing. My heart sang. We hugged for a long while before picking up her luggage and heading to my home in Lathrup Village. The afternoon sun began to fade. A late-winter storm was blowing in from Canada. We had a simple dinner, just the two of us, and afterward sat on the couch facing the fireplace in the living room. The flames sparked and crackled. I put my arm around Erica. She moved closer to me. We gazed out the window and watched the snow gently fall. Snowflakes glistened in the moonlight. The warmth of the fireplace, the warmth of Erica next to me, the quiet of the evening.

"No music?" asked Erica.

"Well, I was just going to suggest that. You choose."

"I'd choose something by Kem."

I smiled and said, "We've heard enough of him. Let's go with Musiq Soulchild."

"No argument here."

Of course, "So Beautiful" was the choice. Then Luther's *The Night I Fell in Love* felt like the right album. "Other Side of the World" felt like the right song. The story is about how love, once on the other side of the world, has come to live in our very midst. "Love Won't Let Me Wait," from Luther's *Any Love* album, another song where he channeled sweet desire, called to us both.

The call.

The falling snow.

The roaring fireplace.

The time was right. The time had come.

It was a slow dance, a tender dance, a dance of love where two bodies became one and, at last, we realized what we had long known. Love had brought us here. Love would keep us here. Now the story, consummated with sacred passion, would conceive our first child, the fruit of our love, the proof of love's beauty.

Nine months later, on November 30, 2016, our son Kristoffer was born.

This three-month courtship felt like forever, and yet, looking back, it was lightning fast. I had met Erica in November 2015, and by June 2016, I was looking for a house for us in Georgia. That's how sure I was.

Erica had a bit more hesitancy. I understood. She had concerns that the crazy world of show business could be more than she had bargained for.

On the other hand, I knew the moment of truth had arrived.

"I have no plan B," I told her.

"I don't have alternate plans, but I have fears."

"About what?"

"Being hasty."

"I think you already made that decision when you bought the VIP ticket to meet me."

"Literally, I was just following a dream, Kem. I met you in spirit before I met you in flesh. I'd never dreamed about meeting a man before. But that doesn't mean the fear has gone away."

"What are you afraid of now?" I asked.

"The dream not coming true."

"It already has come true."

"Or once coming true," said Erica, "disappearing. Vanishing into thin air."

"I'm right here. I'm not disappearing. I'm not vanishing. I'm no longer a dream. I'm a reality. Together, we're creating a new reality."

My formal proposal came at Christians for Change, the same church where we had gone during our first date. Erica's formal response, for which I'm eternally grateful, was a soft-spoken but firmly stated yes.

We were swept up by the events, swept up by the energy of the absolute rightness of our union. In what seemed the blink of an eye, I left Detroit, and our beautifully blended family was living in a large, comfortable home in a small community twenty-five miles southwest of Atlanta. I wanted Erica to be close to her family.

A few days before she had a fitting for her wedding dress, we learned she was pregnant with our second child, our daughter Trinity, who was born on October 6, 2019. A month later, our wedding unfolded like another dream: Maui awash in blue—deep ocean blue, light blue sky; fragrant red roses, purple lilacs, white lilies; our handsome groomsmen, our lovely bridesmaids; Erica in an exquisite long veil and trained gown sparkling with golden light; the warm and welcoming presence of our family and all our precious children—Troi, Laylah, Alex, Kristoffer, and newborn Trinity.

I sang "Share My Life"—a prophecy fulfilled—as I watched my wife-to-be walk down the aisle. Our ministers, Denise Brown and Pastor Stephon Ray Henderson, officiated with loving authority. Musiq Soulchild flew in to sing "So Beautiful" for our first dance as a married couple. Our second was Prince's "Adore." And, naturally, there was Al Jarreau's "We're in This Love Together."

The blessings flowed: On September 5, 2021, our son Israel was born.

The blessings continued to flow.

The COVID pandemic, for all its dire consequences, brought us all closer together. Our domestic life deepened. Being in such close quarters, our blended family blossomed in ways I had not foreseen. We grew more tolerant and appreciative of one another.

I wondered how this new life—a life where for the first time I was completely committed to a woman and to a family—would affect my music. In the past, so many of my songs had been about the yearning for something I had yet to find. Now that I had found it, would my writing be different? What shapes would the new songs take in this new season? Not to mention, how was I going to manage the practical matter of trying to record music? I was displaced from the city, the facilities, and the musicians that, up until this point, had been central to the infrastructure of my creative process.

The writing took a while. It always takes a while. But being home with Erica and the kids gifted me greater patience. I found myself sculpting songs that seemed to me my most soulful since the release, nearly twenty years earlier, of *Kemistry*.

I reflected on where I had been, what I had feared, and came to the realization that what brought me through the darkest periods of my life was love. Maybe that's why scripture tells us to give thanks in all things, the good and the seemingly bad: because they teach us to lean on love. God's love. Love is the only way out, a sentiment that would inform the title of a new song and a new album, *Love Always Wins*.

Yes, the struggle had been intense. And yes, surely I knew the struggles wouldn't just cease to exist. But no matter how severe the struggles or how tempestuous the battle, I felt fortified. I felt something deep in my soul. That something comes down to one ideal, one irrefutable truth, which I believe permeates all of humanity: we all love somebody, and somebody loves us.

ACKNOWLEDGMENTS

─────

I am thankful to God for the journey that has been, the journey that is, and the journey to come.

My soul is rejuvenated daily by the love of my beautiful, patient, spirit-filled wife, Erica, and our wonderful children: Troi, Alexandria, Laylah, Kristoffer, Trinity, and Izzy. Thank you for giving me renewed purpose, getting me out of myself, and making me laugh. Your presence is a healing force in my life.

To my devoted parents, I am so thankful that you were chosen to bring me into this world, to nurture me, to raise me, to discipline me, and to love me. Mom, you remain my inspiration, and Dad, I now know that in many ways you are the man that I aspire to be. I love you both.

My love and gratitude to David Ritz for his patience, his counsel, his insight, and most of all his genius in translating the narrative of my life into the written word.

Thank you, Dana Canedy, for your vision, your encouragement, and your wisdom in gifting me with such an amazing editor in Lashanda Anakwah. She truly has been a capable and steady guide during this entire process and continues to be a blessing.

Thank you, Jonathan Karp, and the entire Simon & Schuster team, for holding the line and allowing me the opportunity to tell my story in such a meaningful and comprehensive way.

ACKNOWLEDGMENTS

The man I am today is a reflection of those who have loved and supported me through different seasons of my life. They include but are in no way limited to: the Hardy family, the Owens family, Michelle Vibber, Mena and Dave, Emily Daniel, Sarah Brutman, Cedric Ross, Brian O'Neal, Sam Donahoo, Toya Hankins, Dr. Denise Brown, Greg Smith, Dave McMurray, Carlos Gunn, Eric and Marilyn Morgeson, Marvet Britto, Renaissance Unity, Marianne Williamson, Lori Crane Hess, Edward Gooch, Michael Brock, Ralph Mitchell, Lawanda Anner, Larry Brandeberry, Arty Erk, Juan Ferrer, Gerald Issac, Rob Loupee, Dr. Sharon Malone and Eric Holder, Tom Joyner, Steve Harvey, Tyler Perry, Kedar Massenburg, Sylvia Rhone, Ethiopia Habtemariam, the Motown Record label, and a host of fans all over the world who are still grooving with me as I continue my search for the lost chord.

DAVID RITZ:

I would like to thank Kem for trusting me with his precious story. Kem is a brilliant collaborator, and I appreciate the thoughtfulness and patience he brought to this project. Deep appreciation to Elizabeth Hardy and Eric Owens, whose insights were illuminating. Further gratitude to Dana Canady and our editor, Lashanda Anakwah. Denise Brown, an inspiration to us all, has supported this undertaking from its very inception. Thanks to my steadfast agent David Vigliano; my wonderful wife, Roberta; my children Alison and Jessica; my grandchildren Charlotte, Alden, Jimmy, and Isaac; my sons-in-law Jim and Henry, and my dear friends Alan, Harry, Tommy, and Herb. All these beautiful people, and so many others, sustain my spirit every day in every way. Praise God.

ABOUT THE AUTHORS

———

KEM is an internationally acclaimed singer-songwriter who has produced platinum and gold records and five number one singles, and won a myriad of prestigious awards. Over the past two decades, he has headlined sold-out tours in the United States and abroad.

DAVID RITZ, cowriter of "Sexual Healing," has collaborated on books with, among many others, Ray Charles, Aretha Franklin, Marvin Gaye, Janet Jackson, BB King, and Willie Nelson.